THE FAMILY Handyman

ULTIMATE
WEEKEND
IMPROVEMENTS

KITCHEN

BATH

GARAGE

YARD & GARDEN

Reader's digest | The Reader's Digest Association Inc.
New York, NY/Montreal

Editorial and Production Team

Vern Johnson, Peggy McDermott, Rick Muscoplat, Mary Schwender, Marcia Roepke

Photography and Illustrations

Ron Chamberlain, Tom Fenenga, Bruce Kieffer, Mike Krivit, Don Mannes, Ramon Moreno, Shawn Nielsen, Doug Oudekerk, Frank Rohrbach III, Eugene Thompson, Bill Zuehlke

Text, photography and illustrations for *Ultimate Weekend Improvements* are based on articles previously published in *The Family Handyman* magazine (2915 Commers Dr., Suite 700, Eagan, MN 55121, familyhandyman.com). For information on advertising in *The Family Handyman* magazine, call (646) 293-6150.

ISBN: 978-1-62145-242-3

THE FAMILY HANDYMAN

Editor in Chief Ken Collier
Project Editor Eric Smith
Design & Layout Diana Boger, Teresa Marrone
Senior Editors Travis Larson, Gary Wentz
Associate Editor Jeff Gorton
Administrative Manager Alice Garrett
Senior Copy Editor Donna Bierbach
VP, Group Publisher Russell S. Ellis

Published by Home Service Publications, Inc., a subsidiary of The Reader's Digest Association, Inc.

PRINTED IN CHINA

1 2 3 4 5 6 7 8 9 10

A NOTE TO OUR READERS: All do-it-yourself activities involve a degree of risk. Skills, materials, tools and site conditions vary widely. Although the editors have made every effort to ensure accuracy, the reader remains responsible for the selection and use of tools, materials and methods. Always obey local codes and laws, follow manufacturer instructions and observe safety precautions.

Contents

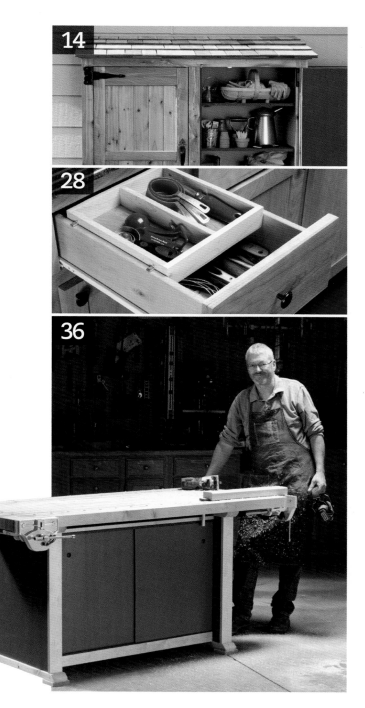

Wire shelving

Wire shelving is popular because of its price, flexibility and ease of installation. Wire shelving can be designed to meet almost any need at a fraction of the cost of a custom built-in system. And while installing wire shelving isn't quite a no-brainer, you don't need to be a master carpenter or own a fully equipped cabinet shop to get it done. We picked the brain of a pro for these tips to help you on your next installation.

WHAT IT TAKES

Time: 1–4 hours
Skill level: Beginner

Buy extra pieces

Even if you're just planning to build one closet shelf, have extra parts on hand. It takes a lot less time to return a few wall clips than it does to stop working to make a special trip to the store for just one. And plans change, so if you decide to add a section of shelving, you'll be prepared.

CLOSET GAUGE

HEAVY GAUGE

Leave the heavy stuff for the garage

For residential jobs, standard wire shelving sold at home centers works fine. Most manufacturers make a heavier-duty product for garage storage, but the regular stuff is plenty strong for the average bedroom, pantry or hall closet. However, if you're going to store a bowling ball collection, you may want to consider upgrading.

BUBBLE STICK

Lay it out with a bubble stick

Use a bubble stick rather than a level. A bubble stick is like a ruler and a level rolled into one. Holding a level against the wall with one hand can be frustrating. Levels are rigid, and they pivot out of place when resting on a stud that's bowed out a bit. A bubble stick has a little flex, so it can ride the imperfections of the wall yet still deliver a straight line. You can get one online.

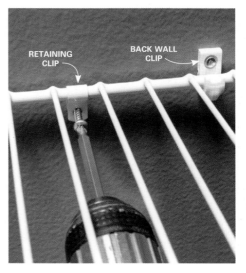

RETAINING CLIP

BACK WALL CLIP

Avoid upheaval

Back wall clips are designed to support the shelf, but if there are a bunch of clothes hanging on the front of the shelf with nothing on top to weigh them down, the back of the shelf can lift. To keep the shelf in place, install a retaining clip in a stud near the middle of the shelf. One clip toward the middle of an 8-ft. shelf is plenty.

TEMPLATE

A bolt cutter works best
Cut your shelving with a bolt cutter. It's quick and easy, and it makes a clean cut. To make room for the cutter, use your feet to hold the shelving off the ground.

Use a template on the end brackets
The pro template used here has a built-in level and allows you to drill the holes without marking them first. At about $200, this is for people who do lots of closet shelving. But if that's you, it's a great investment. You can order one from your local shelving dealer.

ANGLE BRACKET

STUD LOCATION

Space the angle brackets evenly
Consider aesthetics when installing angle brackets. If a shelf only needs one bracket, find the stud closest to the center. If two or three brackets are required, try to space them evenly, making sure that at least one bracket toward the center is hitting a stud.

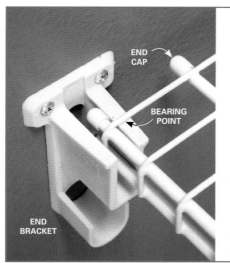

END CAP

BEARING POINT

END BRACKET

Measure an inch short
When cutting the shelf, measure wall to wall, and subtract an inch. This allows for the thickness of the end brackets plus a little wiggle room. It's the top, thinner wire that actually supports the shelf, and one wire per end is enough. Cutting exact lengths will only earn you wall scratches and a trip back to the cutting station.

Pegboard prevents tipping

When installing wire shelving in pantries, it's a good idea to cap the top of the shelves with white 1/4-in. pegboard. This stops the skinnier items from tipping over. Use white zip ties to hold the pegboard in place. Find 4 x 8-ft. sheets at home centers.

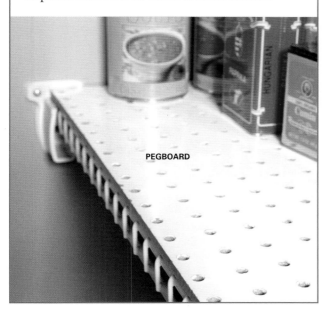

PEGBOARD

CORNER HANGING BAR

BAR HANGER SUPPORT

Hanger sliding freedom

One common complaint about wire shelving is that it restricts the movement of the hangers because the hangers are stuck between the shelves. To avoid that, upgrade to a hanger rod. Most manufacturers make some version of one. A hanger rod allows clothes to slide from one end of the closet to the other, even past an inside corner. This upgrade will add about 30 percent to the cost of the materials on a standard shelf design. Make sure the type of shelving you buy will work with the hanging rod hardware you plan to use.

Back wall clips don't need to hit studs

It may go against your every instinct, but hitting a stud when you're installing the back wall clips slows the process down and isn't necessary. After marking locations, drill a 1/4-in. hole and pop the preloaded pushpin in with a push tool. The push tool has a little indentation in the tip that won't slip off the pin when it's being set in the drywall. The occasional wall clips that do land on studs need to be fastened with a screw instead of a pin. You can order a push tool from your local shelving dealer.

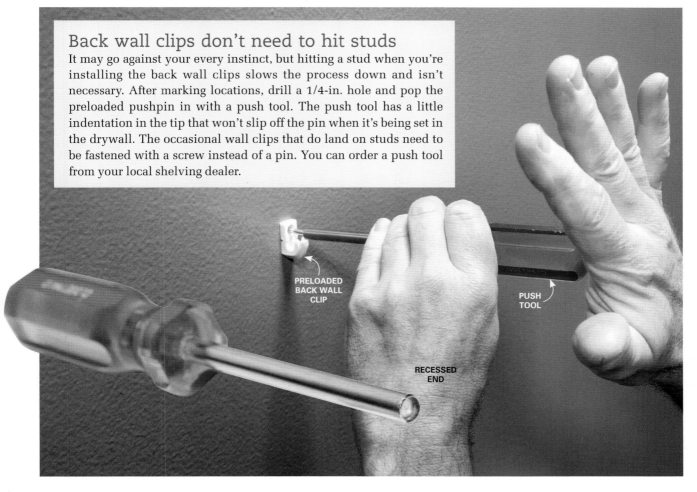

PRELOADED BACK WALL CLIP

PUSH TOOL

RECESSED END

Room divider

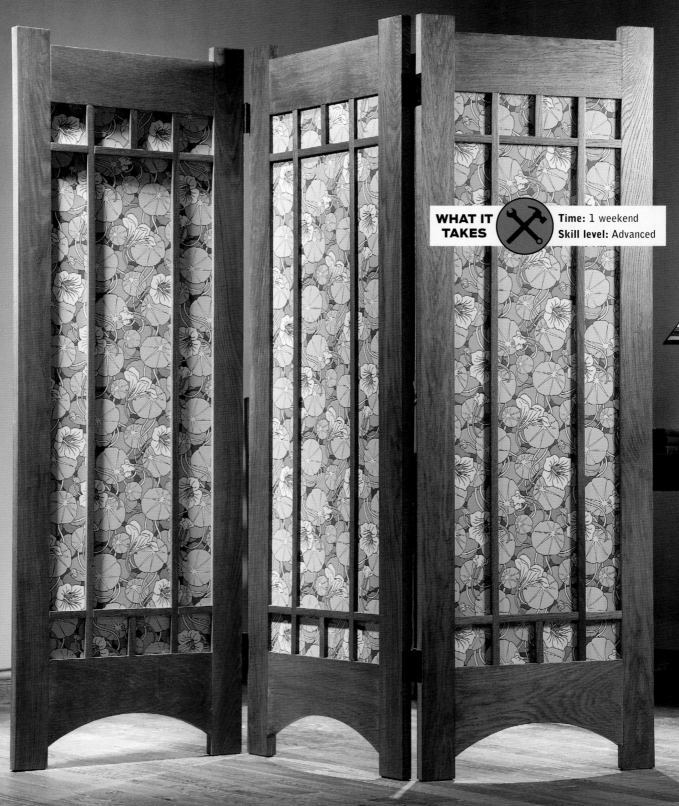

WHAT IT TAKES

Time: 1 weekend
Skill level: Advanced

This room divider has three sections, but you can join as many sections as you like. We used white oak and chose *really* expensive wallpaper to cover the plywood panel, so our materials bill was about $400. You could build it for less using red oak and more reasonable wallpaper. You'll also need a dado blade for your table saw.

An adjustable dado blade wobbles as it spins. Turn the center cam to adjust the amount of wobble and the width of the "dado," that is, the groove. You have to remove your saw's blade guard to use a dado blade, so be extra careful.

Thicker looks better

You could make a divider from standard 3/4-in.-thick boards. But we used 1-1/16-in. stock to give it extra heft and stability. This thicker wood is called "five-quarter" because it's 1-1/4 in. thick before it's planed smooth. You won't find it at home centers, but if you have a hardwood lumberyard in your area, it's sure to have it. You may have to pay extra to have it planed. You can also order online.

Make all the parts

Each of the frames has two stiles (A) and two rails (B and C). These parts are held together with tenons that fit snugly into grooves, or "dadoes," cut into the rails and stiles. Before you can cut the grooves, you need to choose the panel materials so you can get the width of the grooves just right. Take a scrap of 1/4-in. plywood and cover both sides with wallpaper to make a sample block to check the groove width. The perfect groove width for the panels was just a skosh over 1/4 in.

To cut grooves, use an adjustable dado blade in the table saw (also called a "wobble" blade). Plan to spend about a half hour adjusting the width of the cut to get it just right. Depending on the throat plate in your saw, you may need a "zero-clearance" plate.

Cut grooves in the edges of the rails and stiles (Photo 2). Then mortise the ends of the rails (Photo 3). If you've ever made upright cuts like this, you already know how hard—and dangerous—it is without some kind of support. To steady the rails, make a carriage that straddles the saw fence. Don't forget to adjust the saw fence so that the end grooves will align perfectly with the others. Complete the bottom rail with an arch (Photo 4). Complete the stiles by gluing fillets into the grooves.

Next, make the plywood tenons that hold the frame together. Using the same carriage as before, shave down scraps of plywood until they fit snugly into the grooves. (You should be able to pull the tenon out with your fingers; if you can't, it's too tight.) After shaving the tenon material to the right thickness, cut it to size (see Figure A).

Rip the muntin material on your table saw. The thickness of the muntins depends on the panel material you choose. You can cut the muntins

ZERO-CLEARANCE THROAT PLATE

1 **Set up the dado blade.** Set the height of the blade using a 3/4-in. block of wood. Set the width of the cut by adjusting the blade, making a test cut and then readjusting. Then position the fence so the cut is centered on the board and test again.

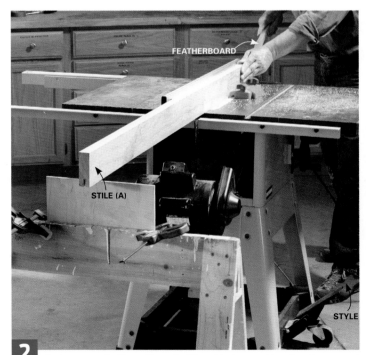

FEATHERBOARD

STILE (A)

STYLE

2 **Cut grooves in the rails and stiles.** Mark one side of each part and always cut with the mark facing away from the fence. That way, the grooves will match up perfectly, even if the cut is a hair off center. A featherboard holds the board tight to the fence. Outfeed support is a must.

from oak 1x4s and make them 7/16 in. thick so they will be flush with the rails and stiles.

Finishing and assembly

Prefinish the parts to avoid slopping stain or varnish on the panels. Be careful to keep finish out of the grooves; it will weaken the glue bond.

Here's the assembly process we followed: Glue the tenons to one stile (A) and then apply glue to the rails, tap these pieces together and carefully insert the panel. Next glue the tenons to the opposite ends of the rails, then align the remaining stile. Carefully persuade the panel into the groove and then draw the joints together with clamps. While the glue is setting, cut the muntin strips and glue them to the face of the panel (Photo 7).

Mark the hinge locations and chisel the mortises to the depth of the hinge plate thickness. Pay attention to the direction of the hinges; they're opposite from the left section to the right section. Once the hinges are screwed in place, apply felt strips to the bottoms of the rails and you're ready to set up your room divider.

THE GOLDEN RULE OF GLUE-UP

Before you grab the glue bottle, test-assemble the whole project. You don't want to discover mistakes or misfits after glue is applied.

FENCE CARRIAGE

3 **Mortise the rails.** Build a carriage that rides along the fence to hold the rails upright. You'll need to reposition the fence for this step, but don't change the blade settings.

16"

4 **Mark the arch.** Drill a pencil hole near one end of a stick and nail the other end to a wood scrap. Draw an arch across the lower rail, cut, and then sand the arch smooth.

Figure A
Room divider

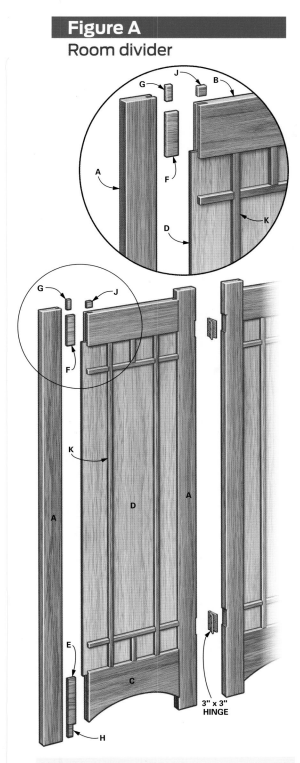

3" x 3" HINGE

Cutting list

KEY	PCS.	SIZE & DESCRIPTION
A	6	1-1/16" x 3-1/2" x 72" stiles
B	3	1-1/16" x 5-1/2" x 18" top rails
C	3	1-1/16" x 8-1/2" x 18" bottom rails
D	3	1/4" x 19-3/8" x 56" plywood panels
E	6	1/4" x 1-1/2" x 5-1/2" tenons
F	6	1/4" x 1-1/2" x 3-1/2" tenons
G	6	1/4" x 3/4" x 1-3/4" fillets
H	6	1/4" x 3/4" x 2-1/4" fillets
J	6	1/4" x 3/4" x 3/4" fillets
K	6	7/16" x 3/4" x 14' muntin bars (trim to fit)

5 **Wallpaper the panels.** Cut the plywood panels to size and prime both sides. When you paste on the wallpaper, let it overhang the panel and trim off the excess.

6 **Put it all together.** Glue both rails to one stile, then insert the panel. Work the panel into the dadoes carefully to prevent wallpaper "roll back." Finally, add the other stile, make sure the whole assembly is square and clamp it together.

7 **Add the muntins.** Glue decorative muntins to the panel. For longer muntins, you may need a weight to hold them down until the glue sets. Don't distort the panel with too much weight.

Mini shed

A convenient
storage locker
for yard gear—
and relief for
your overstuffed
garage

Running out of space for yard and garden tools? The solution is a mini shed on the exterior wall of the garage just for garden tools.

This project cost about $450, but you could save $100 if you used pressure-treated trim boards instead of cedar, and three-tab shingles instead of cedar shingles and felt paper. The project took about 20 hours to build, a few hours at a time. Try to build as much of this project as you can in the comfort of your shop by making each section an individual unit. You can build two sections like this one or stack a whole bunch of them together. This shed is filled with garden tools, but it would also work great for pet supplies, grilling accessories, toys or whatever.

Cut the box components

Start by cutting the sides (A) and backs (B) to the dimensions given in the Cutting List on p. 19. Clamp two sides together, and crosscut them to length at the same time with a circular saw. Crosscut one back at a time with your circular saw set to a 20-degree angle. This will match the angles you'll be cutting on the sides to achieve the slope of the roof. For all your cuts, make sure the surface of the plywood with the least flaws faces inside the locker. Measure down 6 in. from the top of one of the sides and mark the slope of the roof. Again, clamp two sides together and cut them at the same time.

Rip the three shelves (C) down to size and clamp them all together before crosscutting them. Rip the bottoms (D) to size and crosscut them together as well. The only plywood pieces left to cut are the top braces (F).

Cut the cedar parts that will be installed inside the boxes. These include the door stops (L), hinge supports (M) and the door latch blocks (N). Crosscut one of the 12-ft. cedar 1x6s in half, and then rip down the door stops and the hinge supports out of one of the 6-ft. halves. Always square up the factory edges before cutting any of the boards to length.

Sand and paint the inside parts

Paint all the interior parts of this project before assembling them. Fill any voids and holes in

WHAT IT TAKES **Time:** 2 weekends
Skill level: Intermediate

the plywood with wood filler. We spot-sanded the really rough spots with 80-grit paper but didn't sand any of the exterior surfaces.

Only the plywood surfaces that face the inside of the storage locker need painting. Paint all but one of the 3/4-in. sides on the door stops, hinge supports and door latch blocks. The plywood that forms the roof can be painted if you wish, but it really isn't noticeable, and the top braces (F) will be completely covered by trim, so there's no need to paint them. We rolled on a product that was a combination of exterior paint and primer. and were able to get full coverage with one thick coat.

Assemble the boxes

Set the sides next to each other and mark the location of the shelves with a framing square. Then mark a guideline for the screws on the exterior of the sides. we measured up from the bottom of the sides and marked the top line of the shelves at 22-3/4 in., 37-3/4 in. and 51-3/4.

1 **Assemble the boxes.** Paint all the plywood components, then assemble them with self-tapping, trim head screws. Screw one side to the back, then add the shelves and finally the other side.

2 **Trim the sides.** Mount the boxes on their bases, then add trim and siding to the sides that will be exposed. Fasten the trim and siding with construction adhesive, plus a few brads to hold them in place while the adhesive sets.

These measurements are based on some specific items we wanted to store. Make your shelves any height you wish, add more shelves, or eliminate them altogether.

Attach one of the sides to the back with 1-1/2-in. stainless or exterior-grade screws. Save time and buy self-drilling screws that don't require a predrilled hole. Space the screws about 16 in. apart. Once one of the sides is attached, transfer the shelf lines to the back with a framing square. Secure the bottom and the shelves with the same type of 1-1/2-in. screw (Photo 1). Install three screws per shelf side.

Flip the box on its side, and mark a screw guideline on the back of the back. Secure the bottom and shelves to the back with three screws in each. Flip the project on its back again and attach the other side to the back, and then finish securing the bottom and shelves.

The top braces create a solid surface to fasten the top front trim board to. Screw them to the boxes with one screw in the center of each end, and then go back and tack two more 1-1/4-in., 18-gauge brads, one above and one below the screw. Two screws would likely split the plywood.

The hinge supports add extra strength to the trim board that the hinges will be fastened to. Attach the hinge supports and the door stops by driving 1-1/2-in. screws every 16 in. through the plywood sides into the back of the cedar strips. Install the two door catch blocks with two screws driven through the back side. Space them about 6 in. down from the top and up from the bottom, on the back side of the door stop in the box that has no shelves. The door catches on the other side will be fastened to the shelves.

Build and install the base

Cedar is naturally resistant to rot, but it doesn't do so well in direct contact with the ground. That's why we decided to build the base out of pressure-treated wood and keep the cedar trim at the bottom 3/4 in. from the ground. Screw the base fronts, backs and sides (J and K) together with two 3-in. screws in each connection. Attach the boxes to the base with 2-in. exterior grade screws. Install two screws on each of the four sides of the box. Make sure all screws used with treated wood are compatible with treated lumber.

Install the trim and siding on the sides

Cut the side trim board (P) to length and install it with construction adhesive and 1-1/4-in., 18-gauge brads. The brads just hold the board in place while the adhesive dries, so you don't need more than one in each corner and one in the middle.

Create the smaller trim pieces by ripping the 12-ft. cedar (or treated) boards in half. Find the length of the two side trim boards (Q) by setting them on the side bottom trim board and marking the top angle on the back side of the board. Install them with adhesive and two brads every couple of feet. Make the side top trim board (R) by cutting one 20-degree angle and then marking the other angle in place. Install the side center trim board (S) so the top side is 42-3/4 in. off the ground.

For siding, we chose 1/4-in.-thick cedar planks often used as wainscoting (BB). Look for it at home centers near the paneling, not the lumber. If this product isn't available in your area, you could use pine paneling, vinyl siding, fiber cement panels, cedar shingles or whatever is available to you. Just make sure the siding profile is less than 3/4 in. or it will stick out past your trim boards. It just so happened that three of the cedar siding planks we bought fit in between the trim boards on the side without having to be ripped down. There was about a 3/16-in. gap on either side, which we caulked later.

Avoid a big mess by cutting all the siding planks to length and dry-fitting them before applying the adhesive. Tack them in place with 3/4-in. brads (Photo 2). Just shoot a couple of brads at the very end of the planks and a few on the edges. After they're all in, pound each plank flat with a rubber mallet or your fist and add one more brad in the center of each groove. The brads are only holding the siding in place until the adhesive sets up. Now repeat all these steps to build the other box.

Join the boxes

It's time to head outdoors. We created a platform out of pavers. You could also pour a small slab, tamp down some gravel or build a pressure-treated wooden platform. If you build a small platform, make sure it's level; larger patios should always slope away from the building.

Push the boxes into their permanent location and clamp the two sections together. Before fastening them, measure and cut the top plywood (E) so it's flush on all four sides. Temporarily set the top in place to see that it sits flat. Slip composite shims under one or both bases until the top is flat, the fronts are aligned and each side of the unit is relatively plumb. Secure the boxes to each other with eight 1-1/4-in. exterior grade screws, four through each side.

Trim the front

Install the two outside side trim boards (Q) first. Overlap them so they're flush with the trim boards on the sides. Keep them 3/4 in. off the ground like the trim on the sides. These trim boards will be shorter on top than the side trim to accommodate the slope of the roof. Find the length by holding a straightedge on the roof slope and measure up to that. The drip edge (AA) installed under the shingles will overlap all the top trim boards and cover any imperfections. Install the trim boards with 1-1/4-in. brads and construction adhesive.

Cut and install the front bottom trim board (U). It should be flush with the top of the plywood that makes up the bottom of the boxes. Cut and install the top trim board (V). After you cut the center trim board (W) to length, apply the adhesive. Then center it over the door

3 **Add the front trim.** Trim the front after the boxes are attached. Double-check that both door openings are the same size before you permanently attach the center trim board.

stops and tack it on with just a couple of brads to hold it in place (Photo 3).

Build the doors

Start by cutting the four temporary braces (H) that will hold the door slabs in place while you install the trim. Attach the braces to the back of the door stops and hinge supports. One 1-1/4-in. screw through each side will be enough to temporarily hold the doors.

The door slabs (G) sit flush with the door stops and the hinge supports. Cut each door slab so there's at least a 1/4-in. gap around all sides. The gap can be a little bigger, but a smaller gap may cause the doors to bind. Screw the slabs into place with two screws into each temporary brace (Photo 4).

Now install the door trim with construction adhesive and 1-1/4-in. brads. Install the sides first (X), then the tops and bottoms (Y; Photo 5). Leave a 1/4-in. gap between the outside edge of the door trim and the trim on the face of the locker. Install the door center trim board (Z) so the top is 42-3/4 in. up from the ground, the same height as the center trim board on the sides.

Install the hinges before removing the doors. Cheap hinges tend to sag, which makes the doors a real challenge to hang, so buy good ones. These sturdy strap hinges cost $8 each. Center the hinge on the top and bottom door trim. These hinge screws required predrilled holes. Hold the hinges in place and mark all the hole locations

Overall Dimensions: Approx. 79" tall x 55" wide x 18" deep

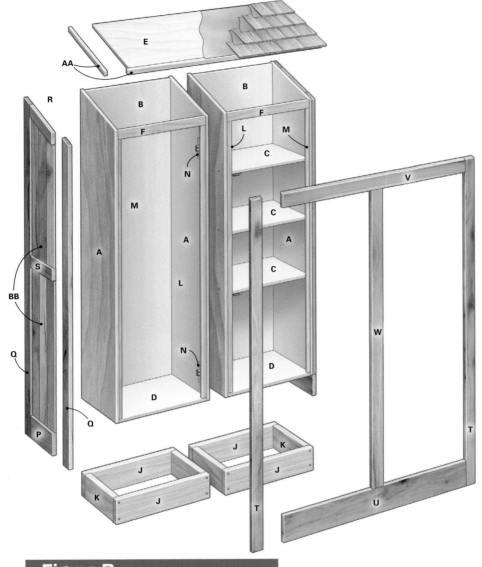

Materials list

ITEM	QTY.
4' x 8' x 3/4" sanded pine plywood	4
1x6 x 12' cedar	6
2x6 x 8' pressure-treated lumber	2
1/4" x 4" x 8' tongue-and-groove cedar paneling (six-pack)	3
Bundle of cedar shingles	1
1-1/4" exterior-grade trim head screws (100-pack)	1
1-1/2" exterior-grade trim head screws (100-pack)	1
2" exterior-grade screws (1-lb. box)	1
3" exterior-grade screws (1-lb. box)	1
1-1/4" 18-gauge brads (small box)	1
3/4" brads (small box)	1
1-1/4" 6d galvanized nails (1-lb. box)	1
Roll of 15-lb. felt paper	1
Construction adhesive (tube)	3
Polyurethane caulking (tube)	2
Composite shims (small bundle)	1
8" decorative T-hinges	4
Door handles	2
Roller door catches	4
1-1/2" fender washers	2
4" structural screws	2
Wood filler (small container)	1
Paint and/or exterior sealant	

Figure C
Door construction

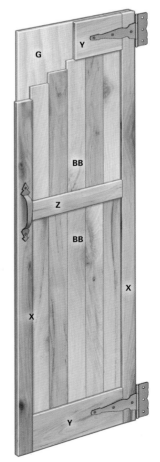

Figure B
3/4" plywood cutting diagram

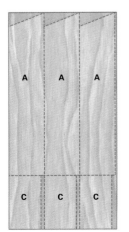
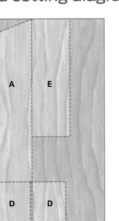
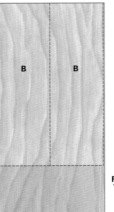
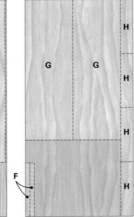

with a pencil. Punch a starter hole in each spot with a nail set before predrilling the holes with a 1/8-in. bit. Mark the depth on the drill bit with a little masking tape so you don't drill too deep.

Once the hinges are installed, take out the screws that hold the slab to the temporary braces, and make sure the doors open and close without binding. Now remove the hinges, and take the doors back to your garage. Doors take a lot of abuse, so install additional 1-1/4-in. screws through the plywood slab into the door trim for a little extra support. Space them every 16 in. or so.

Install the siding the same way you did on the sides. It looks best if the first and last siding planks are close to the same size. We had to rip about 1/4 in. off the first and last pieces to make them come out even. You can just snap a bunch of pieces of siding together, center them over the opening and mark how much to take off each side.

Install the roof

There is a difference between cedar shakes and cedar shingles. We tried using shakes on our first attempt, but they looked too gnarly on such a small surface. Fasten the top plywood with two 1-1/2-in. screws along the outside edges and middle, and four more along both the back and the front edges.

Cover the whole roof with 15-lb. felt paper. Install the

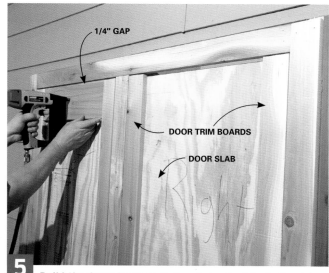

4 **Mount the door slabs.** Screw the door slabs to temporary braces. This will let you build the doors in place for a perfect fit. Keep the screws at least 4 in. from the edge of the slab so they won't get covered up by the trim.

Cutting list

KEY	DIMENSIONS	QTY.	NAME
3/4" BC sanded plywood:			
A	15-3/4" x 72"	4	Sides
B	23-3/4" x 72"	2	Backs
C	14-1/4" x 23-3/4"	3	Shelves
D	15" x 23-3/4"	2	Bottoms
E	17" x 52-1/8"	1	Top*
F	2" x 23-3/4"	2	Top braces
G	21-1/4" x 62-1/4"	2	Door slabs*
H	5-1/4" x 23-1/2"	4	Temporary door brace
*Cut to fit			
Pressure-treated lumber:			
J	1-1/2" x 5-1/2" x 25-1/4"	4	Base fronts and backs
K	1-1/2" x 5-1/2" x 12-3/4"	4	Base sides
Cedar (or pressure-treated):			
L	3/4" x 1-1/4"	2	Door stops*
M	3/4" x 3/4"	2	Hinge supports*
N	3/4" x 1-1/4" x 4"	2	Door latch blocks
P	3/4" x 5-1/2"	2	Side bottom trim boards*
Q	3/4" x 2-3/4"	4	Side trim boards*
R	3/4" x 2-3/4"	2	Side top trim boards*
S	3/4" x 2-3/4"	2	Side center trim boards*
T	3/4" x 2-3/4"	2	Front side trim boards*
U	3/4" x 5-1/2"	1	Front bottom trim board*
V	3/4" x 2-3/4"	1	Front top trim board*
W	3/4" x 2-3/4"	1	Front center trim board*
X	3/4" x 2-3/4"	4	Door side trim boards*
Y	3/4" x 5-1/2"	4	Door top and bottom trim boards*
Z	3/4" x 2-3/4"	2	Door center trim boards*
AA	3/4" x 1-1/8"	3	Drip edge*
BB	1/4" x 3/1/2"		Cedar planks*
*Cut to fit			

5 **Build the doors in place.** Nail and glue the trim to the slabs, leaving an even gap around the edges. Then screw on the hinges, remove the temporary screws in the slabs, and install the siding back in your garage.

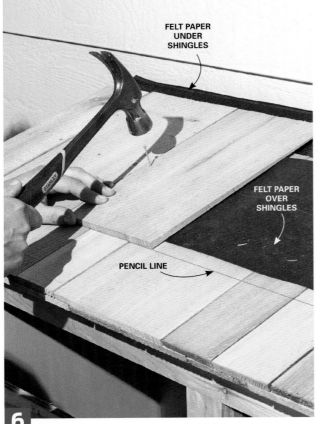

FELT PAPER UNDER SHINGLES

FELT PAPER OVER SHINGLES

PENCIL LINE

6 **Shingle the roof.** Cover the roof with felt paper. Prevent water from leaking between the shingles by covering every row with a strip of additional felt paper.

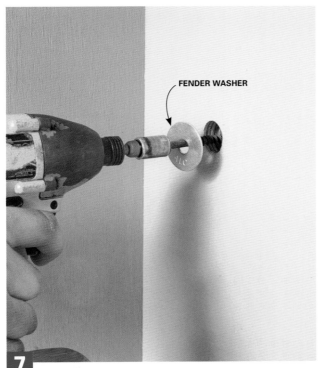

FENDER WASHER

7 **Prevent tipping!** This shallow locker can tip forward easily, so once you've applied your finish to the exterior, fasten the locker to wall studs with a couple of screws. An oversize hole and a fender washer on your screws will allow the locker to move up or down slightly with ground movement.

first row of shingles so they overhang 1-1/2 in. past the trim on the front and sides. Drive in two 1-1/2-in. galvanized 4d nails per shingle about 3/4 in. from each edge and about 1-1/2 in. above the exposure line. Lay down a layer of felt paper about 8 in. wide and cover the whole first row almost to the bottom of the shingles. Install the second row directly over the first, staggering the seams as you go. Install another 8-in. strip of felt paper over this second row about 5-3/4 in. up from the bottom of the shingles. That's an inch higher than the exposure line. In this case, each of the four rows will have a 4-3/4-in. exposure. Use a straightedge and a pencil line to mark each row as you go (Photo 6).

Overlap the rest of the rows with felt paper in the same manner. You'll need to trim the back side of the shingles on the last two rows. It's easier to do this if you pull the locker away from the wall and mark each shingle as you go. The exposed nail heads on the last row will get sealed later on.

Install the drip edge (AA) under the shingles. Install the sides first, then the front. Secure them with construction adhesive and 1-1/4-in. brads spaced every 8 in.

Seal the exterior

Seal the exterior before you push the storage locker back up against the wall and reinstall the doors. Start with a polyurethane caulk similar to the final color of your project. Seal all the areas where the siding meets the trim. Fill any knotholes or voids in the siding and trim, and don't forget to cover the exposed nails on the shingles. Let the caulk dry overnight before applying the finish.

We coated our storage locker with a wood finish made by Sikkens, which darkened the wood just a bit. This product holds up well, but it's also really stinky. Wear a respirator and finish the doors outside. We laid it down with a roller and back-brushed it. Force a little extra sealant into the holes made by the brads. If you don't want your shingles to turn a weathered gray, cover them with sealant as well (We left ours alone). Apply one coat and will add another coat next year.

Finish it up

The profile of this storage locker is tall and thin, so secure the locker to the wall to prevent it from tipping over. Push it back into place and reinstall the shims so it's tight up against the wall and the sides are plumb. Soil can rise and fall in cold climate regions because of the freeze/thaw cycle. To give the unit a little wiggle room, drill a 3/4-in. hole through the back and secure the locker to your garage wall with two 4-in. screws and 1-1/2-in. fender washers (Photo 7), one on each side. An easy way to find the studs in the garage wall is to locate the nails in the siding.

Reinstall the doors and install the door catches. Install them where you attached the support blocks. On the other side, install one underneath the top and bottom shelves. All that's left is to trim off the shims, attach the handles and fill up your locker.

Remote garden storage

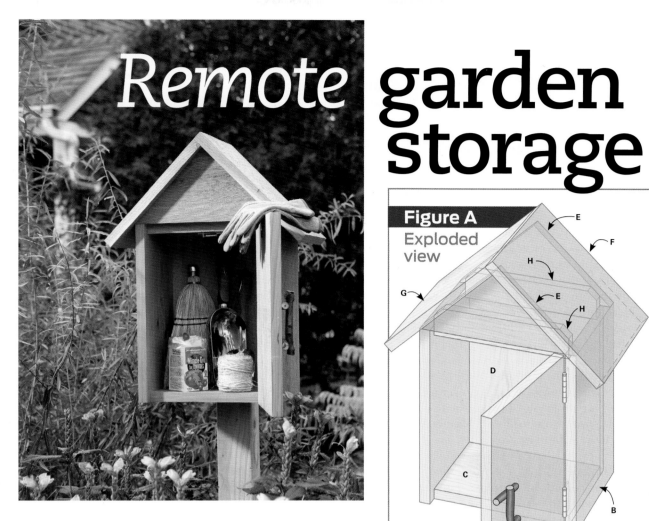

Figure A
Exploded view

Overall dimensions:
23-1/2" H x 18" W x 11-1/4" D

Keep tools and supplies right next to your garden with this small storage house. It only takes a few hours to build, and can be built with pine or rough-sawn cedar as shown here.

Cut flat, dry 1x12s to the sizes in the Cutting list. Nail and glue the sides, base and back together, then attach the rafters and gables.

Fasten the shorter roof panel on one side, leaving 7/8-in. overhangs in the front and back. Caulk the top edge, then nail the long panel on.

Cut the hinge mortises into the door and side and hang the door. Stain or paint the wood inside and out to seal it. Use green branches for the handle, nailing them in place.

Make a rustic door handle from a tree branch. Nail the crosspieces to the door with brad nails, then notch the back of the handle so it sits flat on the crosspieces and nail it in place.

WHAT IT TAKES **Time:** 3 hours
Skill level: Beginner

Materials list

ITEM	QTY.
1x12 x 8' cedar or pine	2
4x4 x 8' post	1
2" x 2" mortise hinges	1 pr.
Magnetic catch	1
1-1/2" galvanized finish nails	1 lb.

Cutting list

KEY	QTY.	SIZE & DESCRIPTION
A	1	11" x 15-3/4" door
B	2	9-1/2" x 15-7/8" sides
C	1	11-1/4" x 8" bottom
D	1	11-1/4" x 15-7/8" back
E	2	12-3/4" x 6-1/2" gables
F	1	11-1/4" x 12-3/4" long roof panel
G	1	11-1/4" x 12" short roof panel
H	2	11-1/4" x 2-1/2" rafters

Note: All dimensions are for 3/4"-thick wood.

Insulate rim joists *and cut heat loss*

In just a couple of hours, you can seal and insulate your rim joists, which are a major source of heat loss in many homes. Properly insulating and air-sealing rim joists takes patience, so most builders simply stuff in some fiberglass and walk away.

If you have an unfinished basement, you can properly insulate the rim joists in two or three hours. (This will also block tiny passages where spiders and other insects enter your basement!) Call your local building inspections department before you begin this project. The inspector may require you to cover the new insulation with drywall (as a fire block) or leave some areas uncovered to allow for termite inspections. You can insulate second-floor rim joists following the same steps shown here if you happen to tear out a ceiling during remodeling.

Rigid foam is the best insulation for rim joists. We chose 2-in.-thick (R-10) "extruded polystyrene" (sold in 4 x 8-ft. sheets). Don't use "expanded polystyrene," which is a less effective air and moisture barrier.

Cut the foam into 8-ft.-long strips 1/8 in. less than the height of the rim joist. A table saw is the fastest way to "rip" these strips, but you can also use a circular saw. Then cut the strips to length to fit between the joists, again cutting them 1/8 in. short (Photo 1). A heavy-duty box cutter is the best knife for making short cuts and trimming foam; the long blade slices cleanly through the foam (a utility knife blade is too short). Use long sections of foam to cover the rim joists that are parallel to the floor joists (Photo 2). Don't worry about cutting the foam for a tight fit around pipes, cables or other obstructions; you can seal large gaps with expanding foam sealant later.

It's important to create an airtight seal around each section of foam using caulk or expanding foam (Photo 2). Otherwise, moist inside air could condense on the cold rim joist. The resulting dampness can lead to mold and rot. If you have a solid concrete foundation, also run a bead of caulk where the sill plate meets the concrete. If you have a concrete block foundation, also seal the openings on top with expanding foam. Stuff a wad of fiberglass insulation into each opening to support the foam as it hardens (see Figure A).

WHAT IT TAKES **Time:** 2 hours **Skill level:** Beginner

FLOOR JOIST · **FOAM INSULATION** · **RIM JOIST** · **BOX CUTTER**

1 Cut rigid foam insulation into strips with a table saw or a circular saw. Cut the strips to fit between floor joists using a box cutter.

CAULK · **EXPANDING FOAM**

2 Run a bead of acrylic caulk around each section of foam to form an airtight barrier. Fill gaps larger than 1/4 in. with expanding foam sealant.

Install smarter switches

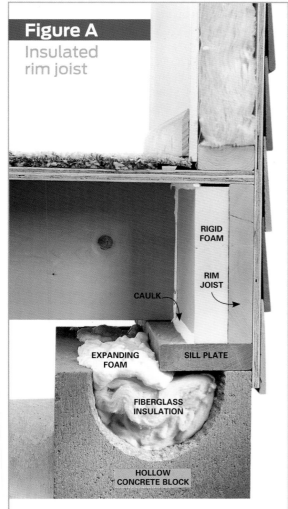

RIGID FOAM

RIM JOIST

CAULK

EXPANDING FOAM

SILL PLATE

FIBERGLASS INSULATION

HOLLOW CONCRETE BLOCK

Airtight insulation reduces heat loss through the rim joist. Fiberglass insulation and expanding foam seal the open top of hollow concrete blocks.

Motion sensors (occupancy sensors) automatically turn lights on and off so you only get (and pay for!) light when you need it (photo above). Some motion sensors need to be manually turned on but turn off automatically. They're great for bedrooms because they won't turn on when you move in your sleep.

Some switches are installed in junction boxes; others are wireless. You can also buy light fixtures with built-in motion sensors. You'll need special motion sensors for electronic ballasts that control CFLs. Special-order them at home centers or search online.

Use timers to control bath fans so the fan will run for a preset time to air out the room and then automatically turn off (photo at right). You can set the length of time you want the fan to run. Be sure the timer you buy is rated for motors, not just lighting (check the label).

30 min.

15 min.

10 min.

5 min.

12:00

A timer lets you turn on the fan and walk away. You don't have to remember to come back later and turn it off.

Organize
your garage
in one morning

There are lots of ways to create more storage space in your garage, but you won't find another system that's as simple, inexpensive or versatile as this one. It begins with a layer of plywood fastened over drywall or bare studs. Then you just screw on a variety of hooks, hangers, shelves and baskets to suit your needs. That's it. The plywood base lets you quickly mount any kind of storage hardware in any spot—no searching for studs. And because you can place hardware wherever you want (not only at studs), you can arrange items close together to make the most of your wall space. As your needs change, you'll appreciate the versatility of this storage wall too; just unscrew shelves or hooks to rearrange the whole system.

Shown here are three types of storage supplies: wire shelves, wire baskets, and a variety of hooks, hangers and brackets (see p. 25). Selecting and arranging these items to suit your stuff can be the most time-consuming part of this project. To simplify that task, outline the dimensions of your plywood wall on the garage floor with masking tape. Then gather all the stuff you want to store and lay it out on your outline. Arrange and rearrange items to make the most of your wall space. Then make a list of the hardware you need before you head off to the hardware store or home center.

Money, materials and planning

The total materials bill for the 6 x 16-ft. section of wall shown here was about $200. Everything you need is available at home centers. Shown is 3/4-in.-thick "BC"

WHAT IT TAKES — **Time:** 4 hours — **Skill level:** Beginner

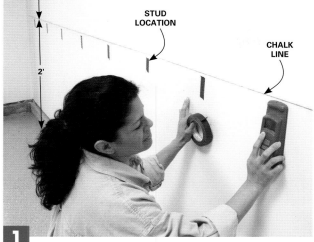

1 Snap a level chalk line to mark the bottom edge of the plywood. Locate studs and mark them with masking tape.

Labels on image 2: 7' TO CEILING, 2', STUD LOCATION, CHALK LINE

2 Screw temporary blocks to studs at the chalk line. Start a few screws in the plywood. Rest the plywood on the blocks and screw it to studs.

Labels on image 1: 2-1/4" SCREW, SUPPORT BLOCK

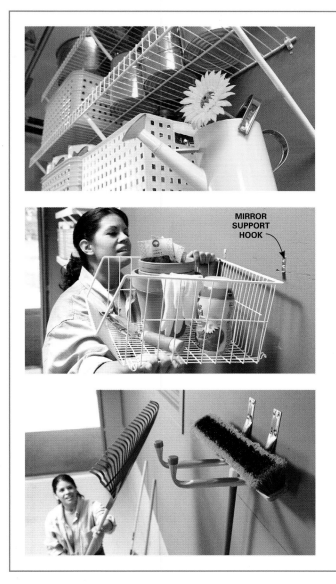

Label on image 3: MIRROR SUPPORT HOOK

Storage supplies for every need

Wire closet shelves are sturdy and inexpensive, and they don't collect dust like solid shelving. They come in lengths up to 12 ft. and you can cut them to any length using a hacksaw or bolt cutters. Standard depths are 12, 16 and 20 in. You'll get more shelving for your money by cutting up long sections than by buying shorter sections. Brackets and support clips (Photo 4) are usually sold separately.

Wire or plastic baskets are perfect for items that won't stay put on shelves (like balls and other toys) and for bags of charcoal or fertilizer that tend to tip and spill. They're also convenient because they're mobile; hang them on hooks and you can lift them off to tote all your tools or toys to the garden or sandbox. You'll find baskets in a variety of shapes and sizes at home centers and discount stores. You can use just about any type of hook to hang baskets. Heavy-duty mirror supports fit these baskets perfectly.

Hooks, hangers and brackets handle all the odd items that don't fit on shelves or in baskets. Basic hooks are often labeled for a specific purpose, but you can use them in other ways. Big "ladder brackets," for example, can hold several long-handled tools. "Ceiling hooks" for bikes also work on walls. Don't write off the wall area below the plywood—it's prime space for items that don't protrude far from the wall. We drove hooks into studs to hang an extension ladder.

3 Set the upper course of plywood in place and screw it to studs. Stagger the vertical joints between the upper and lower courses.

VERTICAL JOINT

12" SCREW SPACING

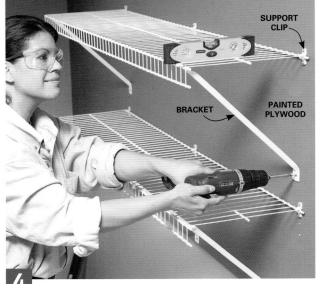

4 Fasten the back edge of shelves with plastic clips. Set a level on the shelf and install the end brackets. Then add center brackets every 2 ft.

SUPPORT CLIP

BRACKET

PAINTED PLYWOOD

grade plywood, which has one side sanded smooth. You could save a few bucks by using 3/4-in. OSB "chip board" (oriented strand board) or MDF (medium-density fiberboard). But don't use particleboard; it doesn't hold screws well enough for this job. Aside from standard hand tools, all you need to complete this project is a drill to drive screws and a circular saw to cut plywood. You may also need a helper when handling plywood—full sheets are awkward and heavy.

This project doesn't require much planning; just decide how much of the wall you want to cover with plywood. You can cover an entire wall floor-to-ceiling or cover any section of a wall. In this garage, the lower 3 ft. of wall and upper 18 in. were left uncovered, since those high and low areas are best used for other types of storage. To make the most of the plywood, a course of full-width sheets was combined with a course of sheets cut in half. If your ceiling height is 9 ft. or less, a single 4-ft.-wide course of plywood may suit your needs.

Cover the wall with plywood

When you've determined the starting height of the plywood, measure up from the floor at one end of the wall and drive a nail. Then measure down to the nail from the ceiling and use that measurement to make a pencil mark at the other end of the wall. (Don't measure up from the floor, since garage floors often slope.) Hook your chalk line on the nail, stretch it to the pencil mark and snap a line (Photo 1).

Cut the first sheet of plywood to length so it ends at the center of a stud. Place the end you cut in the corner. That way the factory-cut edge will form a tight joint with the factory edge of the next sheet. Be sure to place the rough side of the plywood against the wall. Fasten the plywood with 10d finish nails or screws that are at least 2-1/4 in. long (Photo 2). Shown here are trim screws, which have small heads that are easy to cover with a dab of spackling compound. Drive screws or nails every 12

5 Acrylic photo frames make great label holders. Just slip in your labels and hot-glue the frames to wire baskets. Frames are sold at office supply and discount stores.

Garden

Sports

Beach

Lawn

Auto

in. into each stud. If you add a second course of plywood above the first as shown (Photo 3), you'll have to cut the plywood to width. You can use a circular saw, but a table saw gives you faster, straighter cuts. Some home centers and lumberyards cut plywood for free or for a small charge.

With all the plywood in place, go ahead and mount the hardware, or take a few extra steps to dress up the wall first: You can add 3/4-in. cove molding along the lower edge of the plywood for a neater look and to cover up the chalk line and screw holes left by the support blocks. You can also frame the window trim with doorstop molding to hide small gaps between the trim and the plywood. Caulk gaps between the sheets of plywood and fill screw holes. Finally, prime the plywood, lightly sand it with 100-grit sandpaper and paint it.

Handy hooks

When you're out shopping, you might find elaborate hangers designed to hold specific toys and tools. These specialty hooks are nice, but you don't have to spend $10 or more just to hang a bike or garden tools. With a little ingenuity, you can hang just about anything on simple screw-in hooks that typically cost a dollar or two. You can place hooks anywhere on your plywood wall. If you don't put them on the plywood, be sure to locate them at studs.

Drill a hole at a 45-degree angle and turn in a screw hook to hang a bicycle by the front wheel.

Hang ladders on hooks below the plywood for easy access.

More projects online

If you're looking for more garage storage projects, be sure to visit familyhandyman.com and search for "garage storage." Here are just a few of the projects you'll find: a hang-it-all storage wall, nifty rotating shelves and an above-your-head shelf system that holds a ton! So if you don't see anything that will work for you here, head to the Web!

Organize *your* kitchen

Perfect place for lids

You can mount a drawer for pot lids under your pot shelf—or under any other cabinet shelf. Before you remove the shelf, put some pencil marks on it to indicate the width of the cabinet opening at its narrowest point (usually at the hinges). Your drawer front and slides can't extend beyond those marks (or you'll spend hours building a drawer that won't open). Then remove the shelf. If it's made from particleboard, We recommend that you replace it with 3/4-in. plywood and transfer the marks to the new shelf. If you can build a simple drawer box, the rest will be easy.

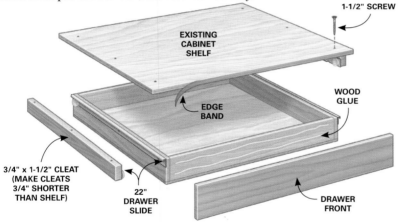

1-1/2" SCREW

EXISTING CABINET SHELF

EDGE BAND

WOOD GLUE

3/4" x 1-1/2" CLEAT (MAKE CLEATS 3/4" SHORTER THAN SHELF)

22" DRAWER SLIDE

DRAWER FRONT

Building notes

- All the wood projects shown here are finished with Minwax Wipe-On Poly.
- Unless otherwise noted, all the materials for these projects are available at home centers.
- If you want to cover plywood edges with iron-on edge band, find how-to help at familyhandyman.com (search for "edge band").
- Several of these projects require joining 1/2-in.-thick wood parts. You can do that with a brad nailer, but if your aim is a smidgen off, you'll blow a nail out the side of the part. Trim-head screws are safer. Their thin shanks won't split thin wood (as long as you drill pilot holes), and their small heads are easy to hide with filler (or ignore).

TRIM-HEAD SCREWS

Hidden cutting board

The secret to this project is "rare earth" magnets. The ones we used are just 5/32 in. in diameter and 1/8 in. tall. Browse online to find lots of shapes and sizes. Implant magnets at the corners of your cutting board and add more if needed.

Make the metal plate under the cabinet larger than the cutting board so the board will be easy to put away. Glue the sheet metal to plywood with spray adhesive. Drill holes near the corners and screw it to the underside of a cabinet.

UNDERSIDE OF UPPER CABINET

1/4" PLYWOOD

SHEET METAL (GLUE TO PLYWOOD)

CUTTING BOARD

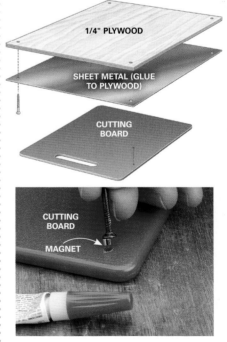

CUTTING BOARD

MAGNET

Magnetize your cutting board. Drill holes sized for the magnets and drop in a dab of super glue. Insert the magnets with a nail head. Slide the nail sideways to release the magnet.

Drawer in a drawer

Deep drawers often contain a jumbled pile of interlocking utensils. One solution is a sliding tray that creates two shallower spaces. Make it 1/8 in. narrower than the drawer box, about half the length and any depth you want (ours is 1-3/4 in. deep). When you position the holes for the adjustable shelf supports, don't rely on measurements and arithmetic. Instead, position the tray inside the drawer box at least 1/8 in. lower than the cabinet opening and make a mark on the tray. Our shelf supports fit tightly into the holes, but yours may require a little super glue.

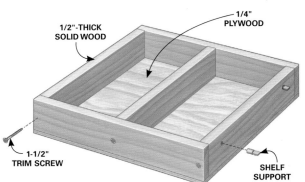

1/4" PLYWOOD

1/2"-THICK SOLID WOOD

1-1/2" TRIM SCREW

SHELF SUPPORT

SHELF SUPPORT

Add a divider for upright storage

Who knows why the pan or tray you need is always the one at the bottom of the pile. But we do know the solution: Store large, flat stuff on edge rather than stacked up. That way, you can slide out whichever pan you need. Cut 3/4-in. plywood to match the depth of the cabinet, but make it at least an inch taller than the opening so you can fasten it to the face frame as shown. Drill shelf support holes that match the existing holes inside the cabinet. Finally, cut the old shelf to fit the new space.

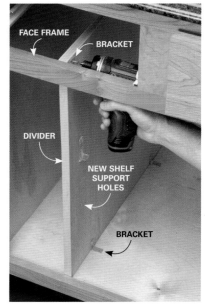

FACE FRAME

BRACKET

DIVIDER

NEW SHELF SUPPORT HOLES

BRACKET

Fasten the divider with brackets. Screw two brackets to the cabinet floor; one to the face frame and one to the back wall of the cabinet (not shown).

Rollout storage panel

If you know how to mount a slab of plywood on drawer slides, you can take advantage of all the nifty shelves, hooks and holders sold at home centers. It's easy as long as you remember two critical things: First, make sure the drawer slides are parallel (see photo below). Second, make your cleats thick enough so that the slides will clear the cabinet door hinges. (We glued 1/2-in. plywood to 3/4-in. plywood to make our cleats.)

To install the panel in the cabinet, reassemble the slides. Hold the whole assembly against the cabinet wall and slide the panel out about 4 in. Drive screws through the cleats at the rear, then slide the panel out completely and drive screws at the front.

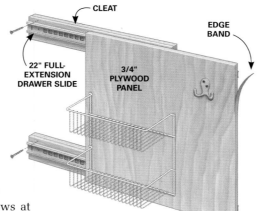

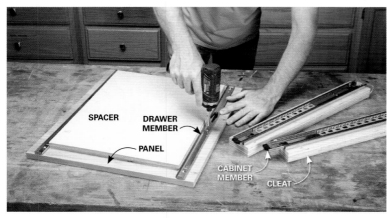

Mount the slides. They have to be absolutely parallel for smooth operation. So place a plywood spacer between the drawer members as you screw them to the panel. Screw the cabinet members to cleats.

Convenient cutting board

The slickest way to store a cutting board for instant access is shown on p. 29. But that only works for cutting boards less than 10-1/2 in. wide. For larger boards, mount a rack on a cabinet door. We used a sheet of 1/4-in.-thick acrylic plastic, but plywood would also work. You can cut acrylic with a table saw or circular saw as long as you cut slowly. Knock off the sharp edges with sandpaper. Also round the lower corners with a belt sander. For spacers, we used No. 14-8 crimp sleeves (in the electrical aisle at home centers). But any type of tube or even blocks of wood would work.

Drop-down tablet tray

This tray will keep your tablet computer off the countertop. As it swings down, it also swings forward, so the tablet isn't hidden under the cabinet.

The mechanism is simple; just make and position the arms exactly as shown here and it will work smoothly. You can cut the aluminum parts and round the corners with a grinder. When closed, the tray is held up by small cabinet door magnets. Clip the plastic ears off the magnets and glue the magnets into place with epoxy. The liner in the tray is a foam placemat cut to fit. Don't worry, small magnets won't harm your tablet; it actually contains magnets.

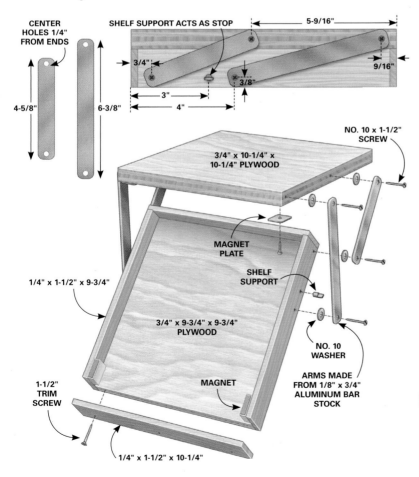

CENTER HOLES 1/4" FROM ENDS

SHELF SUPPORT ACTS AS STOP

5-9/16"

3/4"

9/16"

3"

3/8"

4"

4-5/8"

6-3/8"

3/4" x 10-1/4" x 10-1/4" PLYWOOD

NO. 10 x 1-1/2" SCREW

MAGNET PLATE

SHELF SUPPORT

1/4" x 1-1/2" x 9-3/4"

3/4" x 9-3/4" x 9-3/4" PLYWOOD

NO. 10 WASHER

1-1/2" TRIM SCREW

MAGNET

ARMS MADE FROM 1/8" x 3/4" ALUMINUM BAR STOCK

1/4" x 1-1/2" x 10-1/4"

Instant knife rack

You can size this knife rack to suit any cabinet door and any number of knives. To build it, you just need a table saw and wood scraps. Run the scraps across the saw on edge to cut kerfs. Adjust the blade height to suit the width of the knife blades. You have to remove the saw's blade guard for these cuts, so be extra careful. Also cut a thin strip to act as an end cap. Glue and clamp the kerfed scraps together and sand the knife rack until the joints are flush. To mount it, use two 1-1/4-in. screws and finish washers.

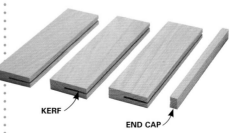

KERF

END CAP

Flip-down paper tray

This tray is perfect for pens and paper. When closed, it's mostly hidden by the cabinet face frame. To install the tray, screw on the hinges first. Then open the cabinet door above and clamp the tray to the underside of the cabinet while you screw the hinges to the cabinet.

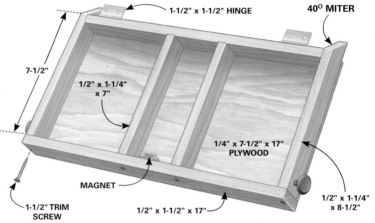

1-1/2" x 1-1/2" HINGE

40° MITER

7-1/2"

1/2" x 1-1/4" x 7"

1/4" x 7-1/2" x 17" PLYWOOD

MAGNET

1-1/2" TRIM SCREW

1/2" x 1-1/2" x 17"

1/2" x 1-1/4" x 8-1/2"

Add a shelf

Most cabinets come with only one or two shelves, leaving a lot of wasted space. So add one (or even two) shelves to your cabinets. All it takes is 3/4-in. plywood and a bag of shelf supports. The supports come in two diameters, so take an existing one to the store to make sure you get the right size.

Hang it high

Double-duty shelf brackets

Shelf brackets designed to support clothes hanger rods aren't just for closets. The rod-holding hook on these brackets comes in handy in the garage and workshop too. You can bend the hook to suit long tools or cords. Closet brackets are sold at home centers and hardware stores.

Under-joist shelf

Create extra storage space by screwing wire closet shelving to joists in your garage or basement. Wire shelving is see-through, so you can easily tell what's up there. Wire shelves are available by the foot in various widths at home centers.

Movable bike rack

Tired of that darn bike hanging in your way? Build this movable bike rack from a 2x4 and a pair of bicycle hooks. Cut four 3-1/2-in. blocks, stack two on top of each other, and screw them together. Now screw them on the end of a 4-ft. 2x4 and repeat the process for the other side. Drill a hole in the middle of the stacked blocks and screw in the bicycle hooks. Lay the rack across your garage ceiling trusses, and hang your bike from the hooks. When you need to get behind the bike, simply slide the entire rack out of the way.

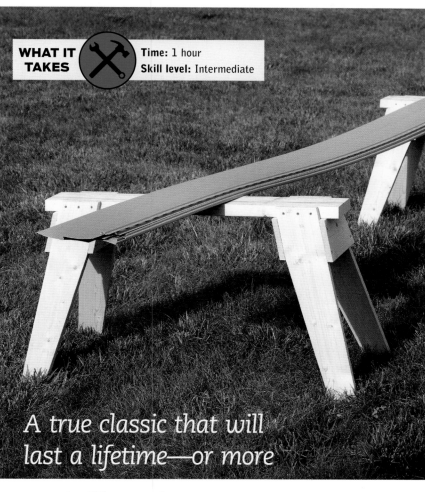
A true classic that will last a lifetime—or more

Set your circular saw to cut at a 13-degree bevel, and cut the legs to length at a 13-degree angle. Mark each piece as you cut it.

Set each sawhorse upright and set something heavy on it so all the legs are sitting nice and flat. Attach the gussets with four 1-5/8-in. screws.

Lifetime sawhorse

Here's a design that's been around for a hundred years—maybe longer. It's low, so you can use your knee to hold down your work. The compound miters make this one a little trickier to build than the others, but if you take one component at a time and label them as you go, in a couple of hours you'll have a pair of sawhorses that your own grandkids will be proud to replicate someday.

To make this horse, you need one 8-ft. 2x6 and two 8-ft. 1x6s.

■ **Top:** Cut the top to length first, then taper the edges on a table or circular saw. All the angles on this horse are 13 degrees. (If you're the superstitious sort, cut your angles at 12.99 degrees.)

■ **Legs:** It helps to cut the legs close to their actual size beforehand so you can hold them up and visualize the direction of the cut and the orientation of the bevel. After cutting the legs to size, reset your circular saw to 90 degrees and taper the legs. Mark the taper line 3-1/2 in. over on the bottom of the leg up to the bottom of the gusset. Lay the top board upside down on a flat surface and attach each leg with three 2-in. screws.

■ **Gussets:** Trim the top and bottom edges of the gusset boards with parallel 13-degree angles. Mark one gusset using the sawhorse and copy the other three from that template.

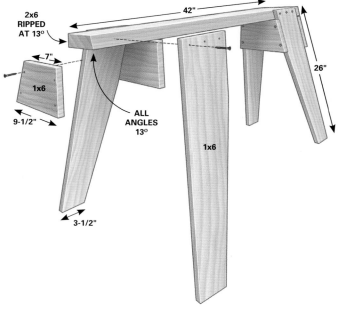

2x6 RIPPED AT 13°

42"

7"

1x6

26"

9-1/2"

ALL ANGLES 13°

1x6

3-1/2"

Bomb-proof woodworking bench

World-class workbench in a weekend

IT DOES IT ALL!

« HOLD LONG STOCK!
Clamp one end in the face vise; hold the other end with a pipe clamp under the bench top.

POUND AWAY! »
The 2-1/4-in.-thick solid maple top will never flinch.

« SECURE BIG STUFF!
An easy-to-build bench jack supports large work.

KEEP IT FLAT! »
A dead-flat top keeps your glue-ups flat and true.

« HOLD STOCK!
The centuries-old bench dog design secures work for machining.

WHAT IT TAKES
Time: 1 weekend
Skill level: Intermediate

If you're looking for a "real" woodworking bench but don't want to spend a year and a thousand bucks building one, here's a great design for you. It'll grow with you as your skills improve; it's flat and solid enough to help you do your best work; and it's sturdy enough that you can proudly pass it on to your grandchildren. One weekend and the simplest of tools are all you need to build it.

Time-tested features

This bench includes the signature features of a traditional woodworking bench: a thick, flat top designed to take a pounding; a tail vise and a face vise, mounted one at each end, for securing stock; and an overhanging top that allows you to clamp stock to the edges.

We eliminated the traditional tool tray because it's more of a housekeeping hassle than an effective place to keep tools. Leaving it off gives you a larger work surface. And since most of us are short on workshop space, we added a cabinet base for storage. The sliding doors are a cinch to make and mount, and they keep the contents free of sawdust.

The base is made from inexpensive 2x4s and plywood. The torsion box legs provide incredibly strong

support and a place to mount trays and hooks to hold bench brushes, electrical cords and tools.

What it costs

You can spend as little as $250 if you mount only one vise (you can add the second later) and you make the top yourself (see "3 Top Options" at left). If you go all out like we did with two vises and a massive solid maple top, your cost will be closer to $800. The 2-1/4-in.-thick maple top we used comes prefinished. Check online for suppliers and prices, or order through a lumberyard. All you have to do is drill the dog holes, mount the vises and you're done. You can also find 1-3/4-in.-thick tops for $200, but if you go this route, you'll need to put spacer blocks under the vises so they fit properly. You can buy unplaned maple for about half the cost of these tops, but you'll face many hours of surfacing, gluing and finishing—and getting the top dead-flat is tough, even for an expert.

To build a bench

Building this bench couldn't be easier. The base is made with 2x4s, fir plywood and a little maple trim. Start with the torsion box legs. Torsion boxes are strong yet don't

3 top options

We used a ready-made, prefinished maple slab purchased online. The 2-1/4-in.-thick top is very flat and stable. You could also use a 1-3/4-in.-thick top. Prices range from $300 to $400, plus shipping.

You can make a top from three sheets of 3/4-in. plywood. Cut them oversize, then glue and screw two of them together and then add the third. Use plenty of screws; they can be removed after the glue is dry. This top probably won't be perfectly flat. Cost: $100.

Use a solid-core exterior door. You can find them wherever recycled building materials are available or buy one at a home center. If you add 1/2-in. plywood as a wear surface, you'll have a 2-1/4-in.-thick top. It should be very flat and stable. Cost: $30 to $60.

1 **Build the torsion box legs.** Assemble a 2x2 frame with screws. Be sure the joints are flush. Run a heavy bead of wood glue, then screw or nail the plywood skin so all edges are flush.

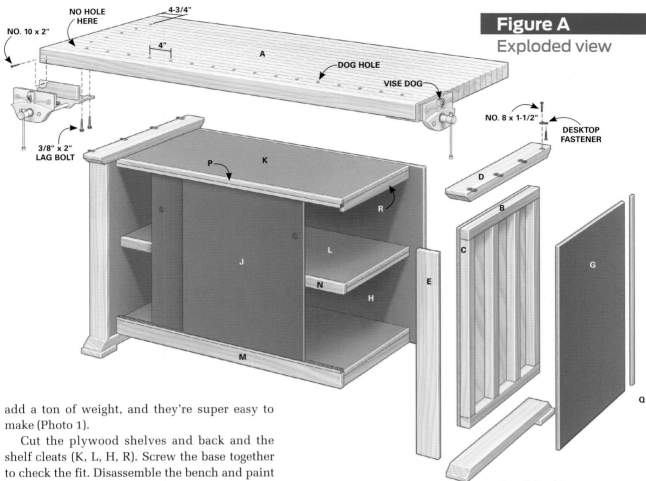

NO HOLE HERE

4-3/4"

NO. 10 x 2"

4"

A

DOG HOLE

VISE DOG

NO. 8 x 1-1/2"

DESKTOP FASTENER

3/8" x 2" LAG BOLT

P   K

R

J

L

N

H

M

D

B

C

E

G

Q

F

Overall dimensions:
30" W x 35" H x 72" L (without vises)

add a ton of weight, and they're super easy to make (Photo 1).

Cut the plywood shelves and back and the shelf cleats (K, L, H, R). Screw the base together to check the fit. Disassemble the bench and paint the pieces. It's a lot easier to paint all the plywood pieces before final assembly. After the paint's dry, attach the shelves to the legs. Cut the 2x4 supports (D). Add the feet to the bottom supports and attach them to the legs with screws. Turn the base upright and attach the back (Photo 2). Add the top supports and the maple trim (M, N, P, Q). The trim piece Q is glued and nailed to the exposed edge of the back. Then secure the door tracks in the cabinet opening to complete the base (Photo 3). Cut the doors to fit.

Now turn your attention to the top. No matter what top you use (see "3 Top Options," p. 38), the following steps are the same. Set the top on a pair of sawhorses and lay out the bench dog holes. Use a guide to drill the holes so they're square to the top (Photo 4). We spaced the holes on 4-in. centers, 4-3/4 in. from the edges. Skip one hole in the front left corner, where it would interfere with the vise.

Flip the top over and mount the vises (Photo 5). Line up the metal dog on the vise with the dog holes in the top. To protect wood that will be

Buyer's guide

Search online for "maple workbench top;" "quick-release vise, 9 jaw"; and desktop fasteners.

Materials list

2-1/4" x 30" x 72" maple top

5 bd. ft. of maple

Sheet of 3/4" plywood

1-1/2 sheets of 1/2" plywood

1/2 sheet of 1/4" plywood

Three 8' 2x4s

Two 9" bench vises

Two packs of desktop fasteners

Cutting list

PART	QTY.	DIMENSION	MATERIAL	DESCRIPTION
A	1	2-1/4" x 30" x 72"	Maple	Top
B	4	1-1/2" x 1-1/2" x 23-1/2"	2x2	Torsion box rails
C	8	1-1/2" x 1-1/2" x 26"	2x2	Torsion box stiles
D	4	1-1/2" x 3-1/2" x 28"	2x4	Top/bottom support
E	2	3/4" x 3" x 29"	Maple/pine	Front trim
F	4	3/4" x 4" x 4"	Maple/pine	Feet
G	4	1/2" x 23-1/2" x 29"	Plywood	Torsion box sides
H	1	1/2" x 29" x 48"	Plywood	Back
J	2	1/4" x 22" x 25-1/2"	Plywood	Doors
K	2	3/4" x 20-1/4" x 43"	Plywood	Top/bottom shelf
L	1	3/4" x 19-1/4" x 43"	Plywood	Middle shelf
M	1	3/4" x 2-1/4" x 43"	Maple/pine	Bottom shelf trim
N	1	3/4" x 1" x 43"	Maple/pine	Middle shelf trim
P	1	3/4" x 3/4" x 43"	Maple/pine	Top shelf trim
Q	2	1/4" x 3/4" x 29"	Maple/pine	Side trim
R	6	3/4" x 1-1/2" x 19"	1x2	Shelf cleats

held in the vise, make wooden faces and attach them to the vise jaws. Use a soft wood such as basswood or pine.

Mount figure-eight or other tabletop fasteners to the top supports. They may need to rest in a shallow hole in the support. These will allow the top to expand and contract without cracking. Get someone to help you set the top onto the base, then secure with screws through the fasteners. That's it. Your bench is ready for your first furniture project!

2 **Attach the back.** Screw the back to the shelves and legs. It's best to paint the plywood surfaces before final assembly.

DIY accessories

Bench jack

The purpose of a bench jack is to support long, wide stock such as a door. To make a jack, screw together a couple of pieces of 3-in. x 36-in. pine or plywood to form a "T." Drill 3/4-in. holes in the face of the jack. Clamp the bench jack in the tail vise, and insert a dowel at the desired height (see photo, p. 37).

Bench dogs

Bench dogs work with the vise to hold stock on the bench surface (see photo, p. 37). They're easy to make. Drill a 1-in.-deep hole in 1-1/2-in. x 1-1/2-in. blocks of hardwood, then epoxy 3/4-in. dowel stock into the holes. To accommodate different stock thicknesses, cut the block to 1/4-in., 1/2-in., 3/4-in., 1-in. and 1-1/2-in. heights.

3 **Mount the door tracks.** Apply a bead of construction adhesive and clamp the door tracks in place. Cut the bottom track about 1/2 in. shorter than the opening. Center the track to leave gaps at each end so the door motion sweeps out accumulated sawdust.

4 **Drill the bench dog holes.** Fit a drill with a 3/4-in. drill bit and drill the dog holes. A drill guide made from a couple of plywood scraps attached at 90 degrees ensures perpendicular holes.

5 **Bolt the vise to the top.** Mount each vise so the metal jaws are slightly below the surface of the wood top. This may require some shimming. I used metal fender washers to fine-tune the vise position.

familyhandyman.com
- To check out our entire collection of workbenches and upgrades, search for "workbench."
- Get your workshop organized! Search for "shop storage."

Upgrade your gas grill to
electronic ignition

If you're tired of replacing worn-out piezo starters, try this fix

It's supposed to be simple: Push the spark igniter on your gas grill and you're fired up and ready for steak. But after a few years, those piezo-style igniters stop working. They bind up and refuse to "click," or they click but don't produce a spark. Rather than replace them every few years with the same trouble-prone style, why not upgrade to a battery-powered spark generator?

You can buy a new-style spark generator and electrode at some home centers and online. You'll probably have to mount it in a different location. That'll mean abandoning the old piezo unit and drilling a new hole. If you're OK with that, grab your drill, bits and a rotary tool and get to work. The entire project takes about one hour from start to fire. Here's how.

First, connect the wires from the existing electrode to the new spark generator and press the button. If you get a spark, the old electrode is good and can stay put. If you don't get a spark (and the battery is installed properly), you'll have to replace the old electrode as well.

Next, find a new location for the generator that's within reach of the electrode wires. Make sure the new generator won't interfere with the gas valves or supply line. Then drill the hole (Photo 1).

The spark generator we bought had side tangs and snap clips to hold it in place. To accommodate those locking features, just cut side grooves in the freshly drilled hole with a rotary tool and a cutoff wheel (Photo 2). Then insert the new spark generator, drop in a new battery, and twist on the push button cap. Connect the electrode wires (Photo 3). Test the unit and get ready to grill.

1 **Make a hole.** Drill a starter hole and double-check for fit and clearance. Then drill the larger hole with a metal-cutting hole saw.

2 **Grind grooves.** Dial your rotary tool up to high speed and use a cutting wheel to cut grooves 180 degrees apart.

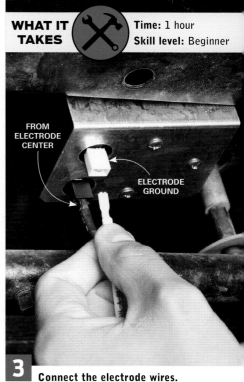

WHAT IT TAKES
Time: 1 hour
Skill level: Beginner

FROM ELECTRODE CENTER

ELECTRODE GROUND

3 **Connect the electrode wires.** Connect the center electrode wire to the positive (+) terminal on the spark generator. Then connect the other wire to the negative (-) terminal.

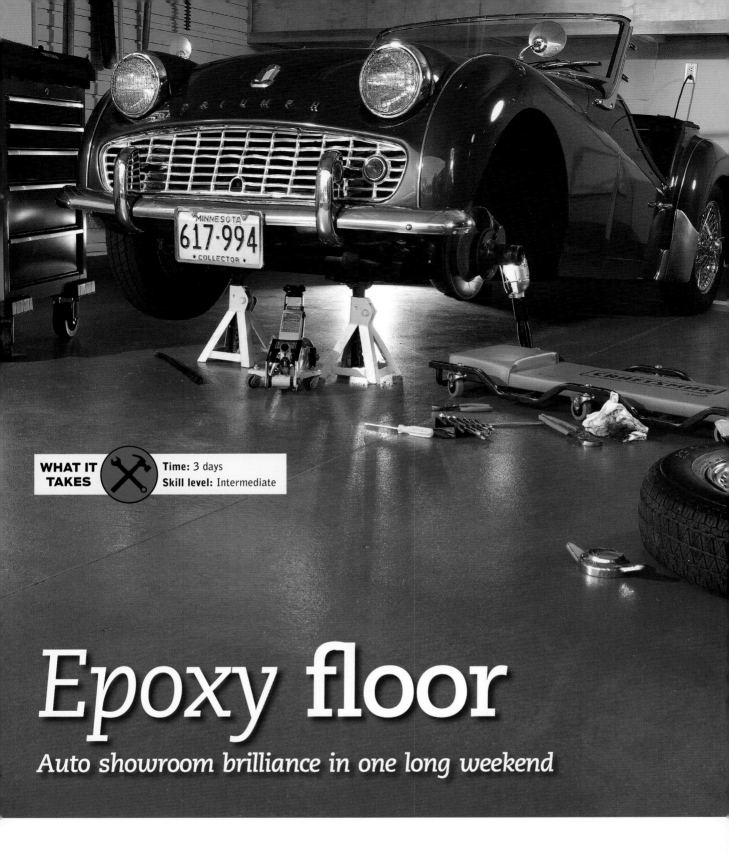

Epoxy floor

Auto showroom brilliance in one long weekend

Imagine pulling onto an auto showroom floor every evening after work. That's the feeling you'll get pulling into your own garage if you give the floor a durable epoxy finish. Epoxy is a tough, long-lasting coating that you paint onto the concrete. It resists grease, oil and many other substances that would ruin ordinary paint. It cleans easily and can be found in a variety of colors (if

you look hard enough), so you can keep your garage floor sparkling clean and attractive for years.

However, the reality of this challenging project is, one, not all concrete floors will hold a coating, and two, preparing concrete can be labor-intensive and tedious. That said, this story will help you assess your concrete's condition, show you how to clean and etch it, and demonstrate how to apply an epoxy surface that will handle car traffic, chemicals, oils, salt and scraping better than any other paint or stain.

As with any other paint job, success lies in the prep work. Plan to spend the first day removing oil spots, cleaning/degreasing the floor, etching it with a mild acid, and scrubbing, vacuuming and rinsing (a lot!). Day two is for filling cracks and applying the first coat of epoxy, which is followed by a second coat on day three.

This job doesn't require many special tools. But to do the best job (and save your back), we recommend that you rent a walk-behind power floor scrubber (Photo 2) with a stiff brush attachment. Brushes work better than scrubbing pads on concrete, but buy two pads if a brush isn't available. Also, rent a wet vacuum if you don't own or have access to one.

Analyze the floor and weather

Before you even consider epoxy paint for your floor, test to determine if dampness is coming up through the concrete from the ground (photo, right). If moisture is evident, your floor isn't suitable for epoxy. Also, forgo the project if a concrete sealer was previously used (you'll know a sealer has been used if water beads up when applied to the surface). If you're dealing with a new slab, you must wait a minimum of 28 days, preferably two months, for the floor to cure and dry thoroughly before applying a garage floor coating. And if you're dealing with a previously painted floor, the best advice is to buff out the old paint or remove it entirely, especially when you're applying a solvent-based epoxy that could soften any that remains (see p. 47).

If your concrete passed these tests, make sure the weekend weather passes too. The temperature of the concrete must be a minimum of 55 degrees F, with an air temperature between 60 and 90 degrees for optimum epoxy curing/drying.

Sorting out epoxy

The final critical decision is what type of epoxy to use. Epoxy floor paints are tough resins that come in two separate parts that you mix together just before you apply them. You can divide them roughly into three types: 100 percent solids, solvent-based and water-based.

The 100 percent solid type is almost pure epoxy; it doesn't contain solvents that evaporate. These products are expensive and difficult to handle because they harden so rapidly. They're best left to the pros.

The solvent-based epoxies typically contain from 40 to 60 percent solids (epoxy). They penetrate and adhere well and are the choice of most pros. And they're often available in a wide range of colors, which is one reason we chose this type for our demonstration. But they do have some drawbacks. The solvents are

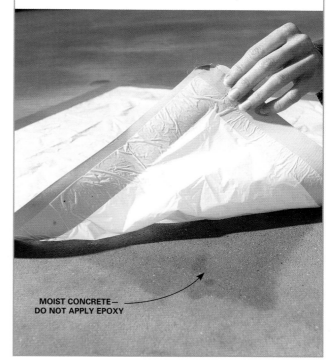

Test your concrete

For a quick preliminary test, lift the corner of a plastic bag that's been taped to the garage floor for 24 hours. If you see moisture under the plastic, don't coat the floor with epoxy; water pressure will break the bond. For a more reliable test, see p. 48.

MOIST CONCRETE—
DO NOT APPLY EPOXY

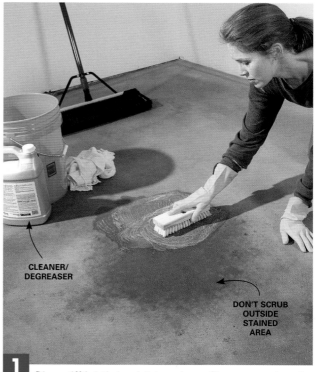

CLEANER/
DEGREASER

DON'T SCRUB
OUTSIDE
STAINED
AREA

1 Dip a stiff-bristle brush into a cleaner/degreaser and scrub oil stains aggressively. Wipe up with cotton rags or paper shop towels. Repeat the procedure until the greasy feel is gone and water droplets no longer bead up on the surface.

ENTIRE FLOOR WET

2 Wet the entire floor with a hose, then scrub back and forth using an electric floor scrubber with a brush attachment (or a coarse scrubbing pad if a brush attachment is unavailable). Pour cleaner/degreaser mixture onto the floor as you go to keep suds going.

SQUEEGEE

WET/DRY VACUUM

3 Push a rubber squeegee along the floor and pool the soap mixture into smaller areas. Vacuum up the solution for proper disposal (see text, p. 45.)

powerful and potentially hazardous; you MUST use a respirator (a 3M 5000 series respirator with an organic vapor/acid gas filter, or the equivalent in another brand). The respirator must fit tightly to your face so you don't breathe the fumes. In addition, you must ventilate the garage well and keep other people away from the odors.

Solvent-based epoxies also may be harder to find. Some paint specialty stores may carry them (Sherwin-Williams, among others), but otherwise you'll have to go to an industrial supply–type store. Check the yellow pages under "Paint, Wholesale & Manufacturers" or "Industrial Equipment & Supplies," or look on the Internet.

The water-based epoxies also have two parts that you mix just before application. And they also typically contain 40 to 60 percent solids. The benefit of this type of epoxy is that there are no hazardous solvent fumes. And at least one brand usually is widely available at home centers.

Whether you're working with solvent- or water-based epoxy, we recommend that you apply two coats to get enough build for long-term wear and durability. "Build" refers to the thickness of the dried epoxy film. Typically, an epoxy with a higher solid content will give a higher build. And, in general, prices tend to reflect the amount of epoxy in the mix—the more epoxy, the higher the build and the higher the price.

For a two-car garage (450 sq. ft.), you'll need 2 to 3 gallons per coat (depending on the percent of solids in the epoxy you buy—read the container). Epoxy for two coats

CAUTION
Always add acid to water, not water to acid, and wear an organic vapor/acid respirator (Photo 7).

WATER/ACID SOLUTION

4 Pour 12 oz. from a bottle of 32 percent muriatic acid (common formulation) into a gallon of water (1 part acid to 10 parts water) in a plastic sprinkler can, then sprinkle evenly over a 10 x 10-ft. area.

can be several hundred dollars. Check the cans for coverage to make sure you buy enough.

Day 1: Floor cleaning

To begin, use a flat-edged shovel or scraper to loosen hardened surface debris, then sweep it out with a stiff-bristle garage broom.

Next, mix up a 5-gallon batch of water and concrete cleaner/degreaser according to label directions (found at home centers and hardware stores).

Once spots are cleaned, power-scrub the entire floor (Photo 2). To clean a two-car garage floor, plan on scrubbing for 20 to 30 minutes (keep the floor wet at all times). Make sure you scrub with a stiff-bristle hand brush along the walls and in the corners where the machine cannot reach. Once you're satisfied with dirt removal, vacuum up the cleaner for proper disposal (Photo 3).

Don't just wash the product down the drive into the storm sewer. The environmental effects of cleaning products can vary widely. Check the product label or call the manufacturer for the proper waste disposal method. We looked up the Material Safety Data Sheet for the product we used (made by Behr) and learned we could pour the waste into the "sanitary sewer" (toilet). Also check the label or call the manufacturer for instructions on safe disposal of all leftover product and containers. When in doubt, call your city or county environmental office.

Before etching concrete with the acid solution (Photo 4), hose down your entire driveway and several feet beyond the sides of the drive. This aids in the final rinse out of the garage so the material will flow more easily down the driveway.

Now sprinkle the 10:1 ratio of water to muriatic acid mixture and power-scrub the floor (with a rinsed brush attachment or new pad; Photos 4 and 5).

Rinsing is key

When you're finished, take your hose and nozzle end and flood the floor with water, spraying the material out of the garage for a good 10 minutes (diluted muriatic acid can be rinsed with large volumes of water into a storm sewer, according to the manufacturer). Rinse off the power scrubber brush/pad, then scrub the wet floor one last time for 5 to 10 minutes. Finally, rinse out the entire floor and driveway two to three more times.

The concrete surface should now feel like fine-grit sandpaper. If not, you need to repeat the acid washing. Finally, to speed the drying process, squeegee out any remaining pooled water, and take a rag and dry any remaining spots, cracks or chipped areas. Leave the garage door open overnight to speed drying.

Day 2: First coat

First thing in the morning, after the floor has dried overnight, fill 1/4-in. cracks and larger, plus holes or spalled areas, with an epoxy crack filler, available at home centers. Use a plastic putty knife to scrape the

5 Power-scrub the 10 x 10-ft. area for 5 to 10 minutes. Repeat sprinkling/scrubbing for each 100-sq.-ft. section, making sure the entire floor stays wet. When you're done, spray a large volume of water on the floor to flush the residue out. Power scrub again, then rinse two or three times. Let the floor dry overnight until it appears white.

MURIATIC ACID

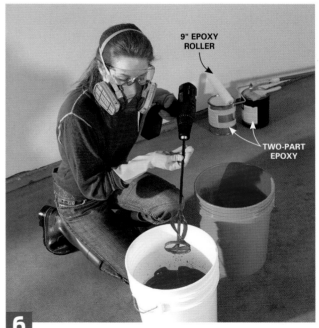

6 Mix the two epoxy components for five minutes using a drill and stirring bit. Then pour the entire contents into a second bucket and repeat the power mix to ensure complete blending of the entire mixture.

9" EPOXY ROLLER

TWO-PART EPOXY

surface level and smooth. Let this dry for four hours (check label directions) before you begin painting your first coat of epoxy.

Mix the correct amount of epoxy (Photo 6) to cover the square footage of your garage floor according to label directions. It's critical that you allow the mixed product to stand undisturbed for the specified time on the label before applying it. You also must apply the entire batch you mixed up before the specified time expires. We used a 40 percent solid, solvent-based epoxy from a local industrial supplier/manufacturer that had to sit for 30 minutes, and the batch had to be used up within 24 hours (and it was offered in almost 20 colors).

While waiting for the crack filler to cure, use a high-quality natural-bristle paint brush and cut in the floor edges (Photo 7). Also, tape the area directly underneath the garage door with masking or duct tape, allowing you to shut the door overnight. This is intended to keep out dust, dirt, pets and children until the floor is dry. And put a "Do Not Enter" sign along with tape across the doorway leading to the garage from the house.

Coating the floor

If you move at a steady pace (Photo 9), you should finish your two-car garage floor in less than one hour.

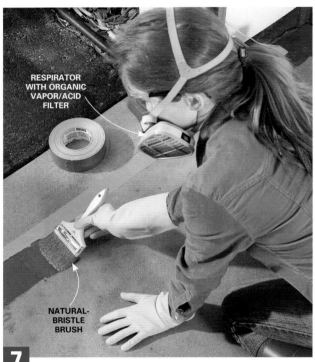

7 Tape the area directly underneath the garage door with duct or masking tape, then brush a 4-in. strip of epoxy along the walls and against the tape.

RESPIRATOR WITH ORGANIC VAPOR/ACID FILTER

NATURAL-BRISTLE BRUSH

8 Dip a 9-in. wide, 3/16-in. short-nap epoxy roller into the bucket so only the bottom half of the roller is covered. (This helps keep epoxy out of the roller.)

9 Paint a big wet "W" pattern that's about 3 to 4 ft. square, then backroll to fill in the pattern—all in 60 seconds. Finish by going over it lightly to remove roller marks.

3'-4'

3'-4'

(Remember not to paint yourself into a corner!) The solvent odors are powerful. Be sure to wear a respirator (Photo 7) and keep the garage door open at least an hour after coating.

Day 3: Second coat

Let the first coat dry overnight, for a minimum of 16 hours (or according to label directions, since epoxy products vary). Add a non-skid product to the epoxy (Photo 10) for the second coat, especially if your vehicles drag snow and moisture into the garage, or you'd feel safer on a less slippery floor. Repeat the "cutting in" and floor painting like the day before (Photos 7 – 9).

Wait another 16 hours (check label directions) after finishing before allowing foot traffic. You can start parking your cars on the floor after approximately three to seven days (depending on the epoxy label directions). A full cure for the floor takes approximately one month.

OOPS!

Despite ardent cleaning and proper epoxy application, we experienced a few dime-size holes where a car tire removed some epoxy. Repainting fixed the problem, but this illustrates the importance of proper prep, enough time for the concrete to dry, and adequate curing time.

> **TIP:**
> A coat of floor wax applied over the top of a cured epoxy floor will make it easier to clean.

10 Let the first coat dry according to label directions. For the second coat, repeat Steps 7 – 9. If you don't want a glossy floor (it's slippery when wet), add a non-skid floor coating additive into the epoxy and stir well to disperse the granules evenly.

NON-SKID ADDITIVE

Epoxy over paint

Epoxy paint can be applied over floor paint or over another coat of epoxy after you prep the surface. Start by renting a floor buffer with a 60-grit sanding screen. Get extra screens and return the unused ones for credit. Run the buffer over the floor to remove loose paint and scuff the surface to create a texture for the epoxy to stick to. Sweep the floor clean. (If you're applying a solvent-based epoxy, follow the manufacturer's directions. You may need to remove the paint.)

Then, just as important, clean the floor with a cleaner/degreaser, which is available at home centers. The cleaner/degreaser will break the molecular bond of the grease so it'll come off the floor. Epoxy won't stick to oil- or grease-contaminated floors. Let the floor dry for a full day, then apply the coat of epoxy.

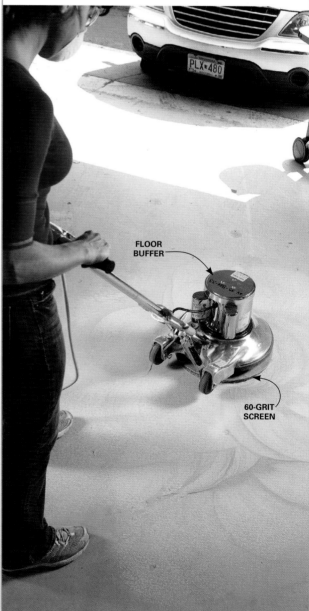

FLOOR BUFFER

60-GRIT SCREEN

Moisture test for garage floors

Before applying an epoxy floor you need to test for slab moisture. For moderately damp slabs, the plastic sheeting test (taping a sheet of plastic film to the concrete and checking for condensation droplets after 24 hours) isn't always 100 percent reliable. A better method is to use calcium chloride–based testing kits (about $50 for the three kits you'll need).

For the most accurate results, conduct the test during the spring when the soil is damp and low humidity is forecast. Dry air draws moisture up through the concrete, so you'll be getting "worst case" results that time of year. Place two of the test kits at least 5 ft. away from walls and the third test kit in the middle of the floor. Follow the surface preparation instructions to the letter. That means you'll have to grind off about 1/32 in. of concrete to remove any surface sealers or hardening agents (Photo 1). Once you've ground off the top layer, use the pH test liquid and strips included in the kit to determine the acidity (pH) level of the freshly exposed concrete. The pH level should be 6.5 to 7. If yours isn't, check with the paint manufacturer to see if its paint will stick.

If the pH level checks out, leave the test sections open to the garage air for 24 hours before starting the test. Place the calcium chloride dish in the test areas and apply the sealing dome (Photo 2). After the chemical absorbs moisture for 60 to 72 hours, cut openings in the domes and remove and seal the dishes. Then mail them off to the testing lab for analysis (included in the kit price).

The maximum amount of water vapor penetration is 3 lbs. per 1,000 sq. ft. If your results show more than that amount, don't even consider applying epoxy or any other paint-type coating to your floor. Instead, live with your old boring concrete or consider a "covering type" floor like plastic tile.

However, if your tests hover around the 3-lb. mark, your results are borderline. Consider calling in a professional testing lab to conduct a more rigid (and accurate) test. Search online for "testing labs."

1 Remove 1/32 in. of the top layer of concrete with an angle grinder and a masonry wheel. Let the area "breathe" for 24 hours before starting the test.

CRACKING EPOXY

Buyer's guide

Search "calcium chloride moisture test kit" for retail and online suppliers.

2 Test for moisture with a calcium chloride dish covered by a plastic dome. When the test is done, cut a hole in the dome and lift the dish straight out so you don't spill the contents. Seal the dish and mail it back to the manufacturer for results.

Stain or seal a concrete floor

KEMIKO CONCRETE STAINS

Concrete stain gives concrete the mottled look of natural stone.

Concrete stain

A stain isn't really a coating but a translucent decorative coloring that soaks into the concrete and creates a pigmented, marbled appearance that resembles natural stone. It typically requires two coats and is applied with a roller or sprayer and then immediately worked into the concrete with a nylon scrubbing brush. The stain itself doesn't protect the concrete, so after it dries, you rinse the surface and then apply one or two coats of urethane sealer to protect against moisture, chemicals and stains (see "urethane sealer" below). Depending on the traffic your floor gets, you may need to wax the sealer annually and touch up the stain and reseal the floor every two years.

Cost: 20¢ to 85¢ per sq. ft. for one coat (not including the price of the urethane topcoat). Available at home centers and on-line dealers.

Concrete sealers

Sealers are like floor paint, but tougher. After paints, they're the least expensive coating and they're very easy to apply with a brush or roller. They dry to a clear satin or semigloss finish depending on the product, and you can also get them tinted. There are water-based and solvent-based versions.

Acrylic/latex sealer

Like floor paint, acrylic/latex sealer is vulnerable to chemicals and isn't as tough as an epoxy, so it'll benefit from an annual protective waxing or reapplication every few years. Acrylic/latex sealer will stick better to a concrete floor than urethane sealer, which is why it's sometimes used as a primer for oil-based floor paint or epoxy.

Cost: 20¢ or less per sq. ft. for one coat; at home centers and online.

Urethane sealer

Urethane sealer is significantly tougher than acrylic/latex sealer, but it doesn't bond well with bare concrete. It provides a clear, high-gloss finish that resists chemicals better than epoxy alone and is less likely to yellow in sunlight, which is why it's used as a seal coat over epoxy and concrete stain. However, urethane sealer is more expensive than acrylic sealer, and solvent-based versions require the use of a respirator during application.

Cost: 25¢ to 50¢ per sq. ft. for one coat depending on the product. Available at home centers and online.

QUIKRETE COMPANIES

Concrete sealers come in clear and tinted versions.

Install a floating wood floor

No glue, no nails, and you can do it in a weekend

Here's a wood floor that's so easy to install you can complete an average-size room in a weekend. The joints just snap together. Simple carpentry skills and a few basic tools are all you need to cut the floorboards and notch them around corners.

In this article, we'll show you how to prepare your room and lay the snap-together flooring. The flooring we're using is similar to snap-together laminate floors

except that it has a surface layer of real wood. The 5/16-in.-thick flooring has specially shaped tongues and grooves that interlock to form a strong tight joint without glue or nails. Once assembled, the entire floor "floats" in one large sheet. You leave a small expansion space all around the edges so the floor can expand and contract with humidity changes.

Wood veneer floors cost $5 to $15 per sq. ft., depending on the species, thickness of the top wood layer and underlayment and trim. Most home centers sell a few types of snap-together floors, but you'll find a better selection and expert advice at your local flooring retailer. You can also buy flooring online.

Before you go shopping, draw a sketch of your room with dimensions. Make note of transitions to other types of flooring and other features like stair landings and exterior doors. Ask your salesperson for help choosing the right transition moldings for these areas.

You'll need a few special tools in addition to basic hand tools like a tape measure, square and utility knife. We purchased an installation kit from the manufacturer that included plastic shims, a tapping block and a last-board puller, but if you're handy you could fabricate these tools. You'll also need a circular saw and a jigsaw to cut the flooring, and a miter box to cut the shoe molding. A table saw and power miter saw would make your job easier but aren't necessary.

WHAT IT TAKES Time: 1 weekend
Skill level: Beginner

1 Test for excess moisture in concrete floors by sealing the edges of a 3-ft. square of plastic sheeting to the floor with duct tape. Wait 24 hours before you peel back the plastic to check for moisture. Water droplets on the plastic or darkened concrete indicate a possible problem with excess moisture. Ask your flooring supplier for advice before installing a wood floor.

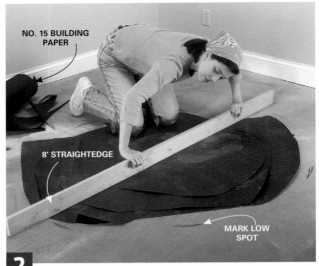

2 Check for low spots in the floor with an 8-ft. straightedge and mark their perimeter with a pencil. Fill depressions less than 1/4 in. deep with layers of building paper. Fill deeper depressions with a hardening-type floor filler available from flooring stores.

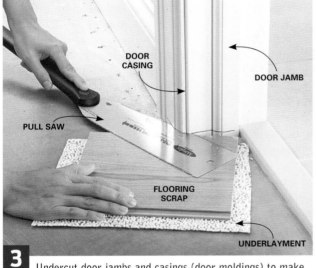

3 Undercut door jambs and casings (door moldings) to make space for the flooring to slip underneath. Guide the saw with a scrap of flooring stacked on a piece of underlayment.

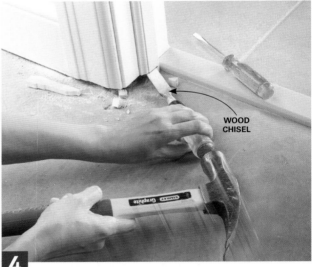

4 Break and pry out the cutoff chunks of jamb and casing with a screwdriver. Use a sharp chisel or utility knife to complete the cut in areas the saw couldn't reach.

Make sure your floor is dry

Don't lay this type of floor over damp concrete or damp crawlspaces. Check all concrete for excess moisture. As a starting point, use the plastic mat test shown in Photo 1. Even though some manufacturers allow it, professional installers we spoke to advised against installing floating floors in kitchens, full or three-quarter baths, or entryways, all areas where they might be subjected to standing water.

Prepare your room for new flooring

You have to make sure the existing floor is smooth and flat before installing a floating floor on top. Clear the old floor, then smooth it by scraping off lumps and sweeping it. Check the floor with an 8-ft. straightedge and mark high spots and depressions. Sand or grind down ridges and fill low spots (Photo 2). Most manufacturers recommend no more than 1/8-in. variation in flatness over an 8-ft. length.

Allowing the floor to expand and contract freely is critical. Leave at least a 3/8-in. expansion space along the edges. You can hide the gap under the baseboards or leave the baseboards in place and cover the gap with shoe

TIP:
A pull saw works great to undercut door jambs and casing (Photo 3). It's difficult to get close enough to the floor with a standard handsaw.

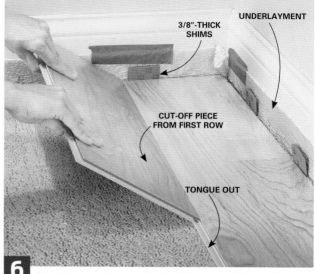

5   Unroll the underlayment and lap it up the baseboards or walls 2 in. Temporarily secure the edges with masking tape. Butt the sheets together and seal the seams with the tape recommended by the manufacturer. Cut the first row of boards narrower if necessary to ensure that the last row of flooring will be at least 2 in. wide. Then start the installation by locking the ends of the first row of flooring together. Measure and cut the last piece to fit, allowing the 3/8-in. expansion space.

6   Start the second row with the leftover cutoff piece from the first row, making sure the end joints are offset at least 12 in. from the end joints in the first row. With the board held at about a 45-degree angle, engage the tongue in the groove. Push in while you rotate the starter piece down toward the floor. The click indicates the pieces have locked together. The joint between boards should draw tight.

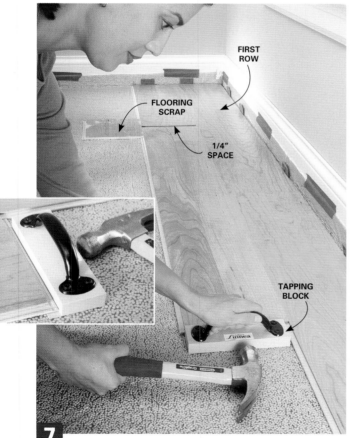

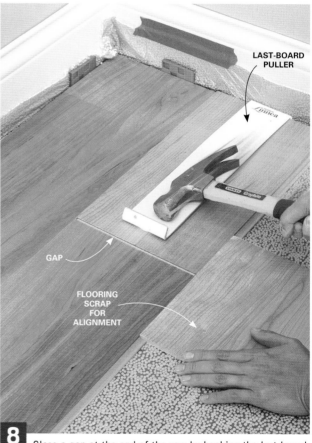

7   Leave a 1/4-in. space between the next full piece of flooring and the previous piece. Snap this piece into the first row. Snap a scrap of flooring across the ends being joined to hold them in alignment while you tap them together. Place the tapping block against the end of the floor piece and tap it with a hammer to close the gap.

8   Close a gap at the end of the row by hooking the last-board puller tool over the end of the plank and tapping it with a hammer to pull the end joints together.

9 Plan ahead when you get near a door jamb. Usually you have to slide the next piece of flooring under the jamb rather than tilt and snap it into place. To accomplish this, you must slice off the locking section of the tongue from the preceding row with a sharp utility knife before installing it.

REMOVE BUMP ON TONGUE

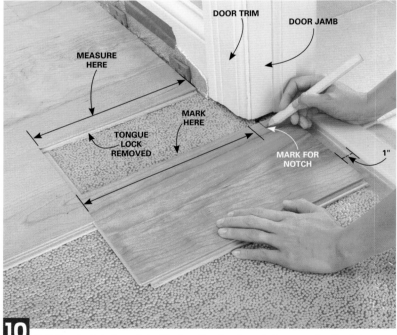

DOOR TRIM

DOOR JAMB

MEASURE HERE

MARK HERE

TONGUE LOCK REMOVED

MARK FOR NOTCH

1"

10 Cut the plank to be notched to length, allowing a 1-in. space for the future transition piece. Align the end with the end of the last plank laid and mark 3/8 in. inside the jamb to make sure the flooring extends under the door trim.

TIP:
If you have wood floors, fix squeaks and tighten loose boards by screwing them to the joists with deck screws before you install your new flooring.

molding or quarter round as we did. Cover the expansion space at openings or transitions to other types of flooring with special transition moldings (Photo 13). Buy these from the dealer.

Finally, saw off the bottoms of door jambs and trim to allow for the flooring to slide underneath (Photo 3). Leaving an expansion gap at exterior doors presents a unique challenge. In older houses, you could carefully remove the threshold and notch it to allow the flooring to slide underneath. For most newer exterior doors, you can butt a square-nosed transition piece against the threshold.

Floating floors must be installed over a thin cushioning pad called underlayment (Photo 5). Underlayment is usually sold in rolls and costs 25¢ to 50¢ per sq. ft. Ask your flooring dealer to suggest the best one for your situation. Some types combine a vapor barrier and padding. Install this type over concrete or other floors where moisture might be a problem. Others reduce sound transmission.

Take extra care when installing underlayment that includes a vapor barrier. Lap the edges up the wall and carefully seal all the seams as recommended by the manufacturer. Keep a roll of tape handy to patch accidental rips and tears as you install the floor.

After the first few rows, installing the floor is a snap

You may have to cut your first row of flooring narrower to make sure the last row is at least 2 in. wide. To figure this, measure across the room and divide by the width of the exposed face on the flooring. The number remaining is the width of the last row. If the remainder is less than 2, cut the first row narrower to make this last row wider. Then continue the installation as shown in Photos 6 – 8.

You can't use the same tilt-and-snap installation technique where the flooring fits under door jambs. You have to slide the flooring together instead. Photos 9 – 12 show how. If the opening requires a transition molding, cut the flooring short to leave space for it (Photo 13).

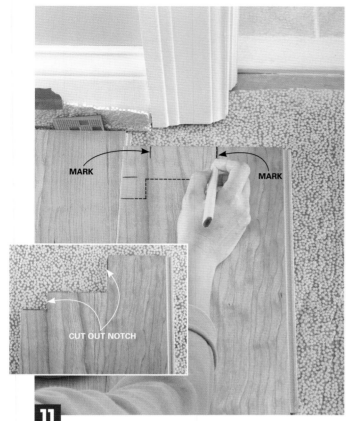

11 Align the flooring lengthwise and mark for the notches in the other direction, allowing for the floor to slide under the door jamb about 3/8 in. Connect the marks with a square and cut out the notch with a jigsaw.

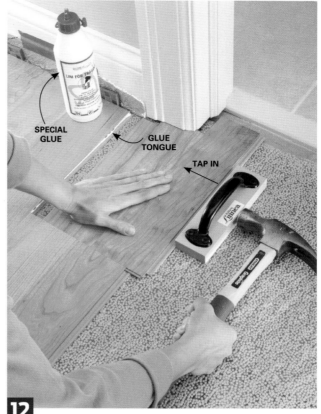

12 Apply a thin bead of the manufacturer's recommended glue along the edge where the portion of the tongue was removed. Slide the notched piece of flooring into place and tighten the glued edge by pounding on the special tapping block.

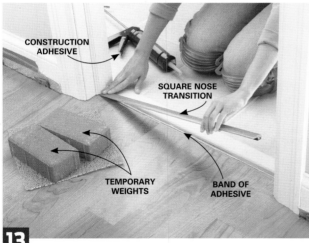

13 Cut a transition molding, in this case a square nose transition, to fit between the door stops or jambs. Spread a bead of construction adhesive only on the area of the floor that will be in contact with the transition piece. Set the transition in place and weight it down overnight.

14 Complete the flooring project by trimming off the protruding underlayment with a utility knife and installing shoe molding. Predrill 1/16-in. holes through the shoe. Then nail the shoe molding to the baseboard with 4d finish nails. Set and fill the nails. Do not nail the shoe molding down into the flooring.

Complete the floor by cutting the last row to the correct width to fit against the wall. Make sure to leave the required expansion space. Finally, reinstall the baseboards if you removed them, or install new quarter-round or shoe molding to cover the expansion space (Photo 14).

Buyer's guide

To find snap-together wood veneer floors, check with your local home center or flooring supplier, or go online and search "wood veneer floors" and "floating wood floors."

Tile over a vinyl floor

If you have a drab vinyl floor in your bathroom or kitchen, chances are you can tile right over it. Ceramic tile requires a stiff base to keep it and the grout from cracking. So the first thing you have to do is check the thickness of your floor. You can usually figure the thickness by pulling up a floor register or removing the door threshold. If the ceiling is open below the floor, you can often tell from where plumbing penetrates the floor. As a last resort, remove the toilet and examine the area around the ring; in the kitchen, pull out the dishwasher or oven and look.

If your floor framing is spaced 16 in. apart, the combination of subfloor plus underlayment (a second layer of plywood directly under the vinyl) should add up to at least 1-1/8 in. If the framing is 24 in. apart, the subfloor and underlayment should add up to 1-1/2 in. If your floor has a vinyl covering with any "give," it probably isn't stiff enough to install tile right over the top. Use tiling Method 1, and add either 1/4- or 1/2-in. cement board to build it up. Keep in mind that in doing so, you'll be raising the floor level 1/2 to 3/4 in. (cement board plus 1/4-in. tile), which means that you'll have to trim the door, raise the vanity or appliances, extend the toilet ring, and make a new transition to the hallway.

If your floor is already stiff enough, you can lay the tile directly over the vinyl using Method 2. With this method you only build your floor up 1/4 in. However, if you choose this method, you should be aware of the possibility that the flooring may contain asbestos.

Asbestos is a known carcinogen that was used in many products including vinyl tile, asphalt tile, sheet flooring and adhesives made until 1980. So if your floor was laid after 1980, it won't contain asbestos unless the installer used older materials. You can clean and sand it to improve tile adhesion, or even tear it out.

However, if you have an older home, and don't know when the floor was laid, do not sand it or disturb it. Simply strip off the grime and old wax with an ammonia-based cleaner. When it's dry, apply a little tile adhesive and let it dry to test for good adhesion. If thin-set mortar with an acrylic additive doesn't stick well, try a mastic-type adhesive. Both are available at home centers and tile stores.

In any case, tighten any loose flooring by screwing down the entire surface with galvanized wood screws spaced every 6 in. Add more screws in obviously loose areas. For complete instructions, visit familyhandyman.com and search for "tile floor."

GROUT

LATEX-MODIFIED THIN-SET

TILE

CEMENT BOARD

SCREW

LATEX-MODIFIED THIN-SET

SCREW

THIN-SET

METHOD 1
Tile with underlayment

FIBERGLASS TAPE

CLEAN OLD VINYL

Whatever your tile, materials and tools cost, double that amount and that's about what a pro would charge for this project.

GROUT
TILE
LATEX-MODIFIED THIN-SET
CLEAN OLD VINYL
SCREW

METHOD 2
Tile without underlayment

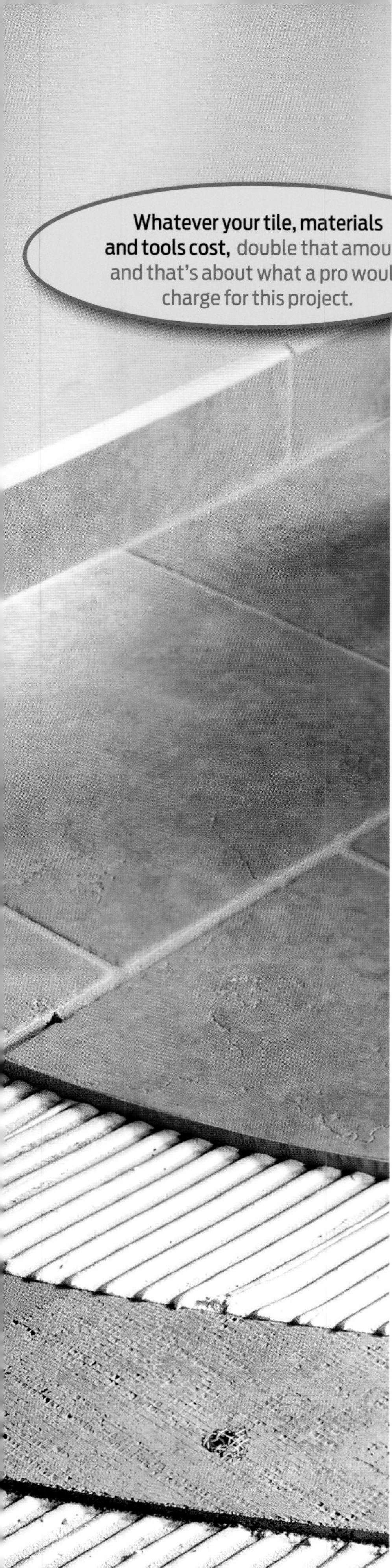

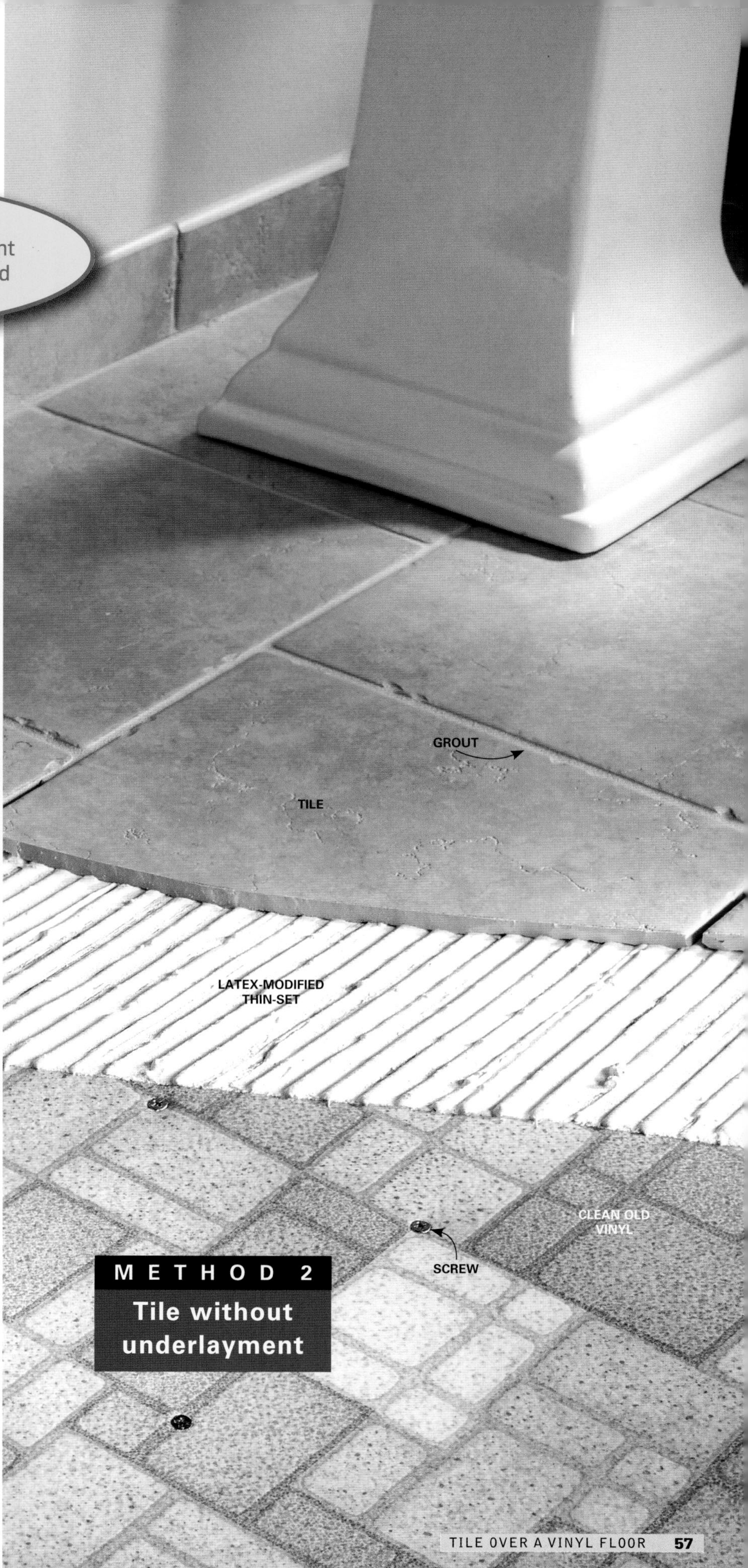

Mosaic tile backsplash

WHAT IT TAKES
Time: 1 weekend
Skill level: Intermediate

Nothing packs more style per square inch than mosaic tile. So if your kitchen's got the blahs, give it a quick infusion of pizzazz with a tile backsplash. Because the small tiles are mounted on 12 x 12-in. sheets, installation is fast. You can install the tile on Saturday and then grout it on Sunday morning.

Professionals charge about $20 per sq. ft. for installing the tile (plus materials), so you'll save $20 for every sheet you install yourself. The sheets cost $5 to more than $20 per sq. ft. at home centers and tile stores.

The total cost for this backsplash was about $200. The sheets of tile shown cost $10 apiece plus adhesive and grout. For an 8-ft. backsplash, you could save about $45 by using a less expensive tile.

Shown here are slate tiles, which sometimes crumble when you cut them. Other types of mosaic tile, especially ceramic tiles, are easier to cut.

Here you'll learn how to install the tile sheets. You'll need basic tile tools, available at home centers and tile stores, including a 3/16-in. trowel and a grout float.

Mosaic tile sheets make it easy to achieve a great backsplash. Layout is a cinch—you can simply cut the mesh backing on the sheets to fit the tile along counters and cabinets. In fact, the hardest part of this or any other tiling project may be choosing the look—the tiles come in a variety of shapes and materials, and many sheets have glass or metallic tiles built in for accents. To add to your options, strips of 4 x 12-in. tiles are available for borders. So you can match the existing look of your kitchen—or try something new!

METALLIC

GLASS

1 Mark a centerline between the upper cabinets so the tiles will be centered under the vent hood. Screw a ledger board to the wall to support the tile.

Labels on image 1: VENT HOOD, TAPE, GAP BETWEEN TAPE AND WALL, LEDGER BOARD

2 Spread a thin layer of mastic adhesive on the wall, starting at the centerline. Spread just enough adhesive for two or three sheets at a time so the adhesive doesn't dry before you set the tile.

Labels on image 2: 3/16" TROWEL, CENTERLINE, OUTLET EXTENDER, MASTIC

You'll also need mastic adhesive, grout and grout sealer. You can rent a wet saw to cut the tiles.

Prepare the walls

Before installing the tile, clean up any grease splatters on the wall (mastic won't adhere to grease). Wipe the stains with a sponge dipped in a mixture of water and mild dishwashing liquid. If you have a lot of stains or they won't come off, wipe on a paint deglosser with a lint-free cloth or abrasive pad so the mastic will adhere. Deglosser is available at paint centers and home centers.

Then mask off the countertops and any upper cabinets that will have tile installed along the side. Leave a 1/4-in. gap between the wall and the tape for the tile (Photo 1). Cover the countertops with newspaper or a drop cloth.

Turn off power to the outlets in the wall and remove the cover plates. Make sure the power is off with a non-contact voltage detector (sold at home centers). Place outlet extenders (sold at home centers) in the outlet boxes. The National Electrical Code requires extenders when the boxes are more than 1/4 in. behind the wall surface. It's easier to put in extenders now and cut tile to fit around them than to add them later if the tile opening

isn't big enough. Set the extenders in place as a guide for placing the tile. You'll remove them later for grouting.

On the wall that backs your range, measure down from the top of the countertop backsplash a distance that's equal to three or four full rows of tile (to avoid cutting the tile) and make a mark. Screw a scrap piece of wood (the ledger board) to the wall at the mark between the cabinets.

The area between the range and the vent hood is usually the largest space on the wall—and certainly the most seen by the cooks in the house—so it'll serve as your starting point for installing the tile. Make a centerline on the wall halfway between the cabinets and under the vent hood (Photo 1). Measure from the centerline to the cabinets. If you'll have to cut tile to fit, move the centerline slightly so you'll only have to cut the mesh backing (at least on one side).

Install and seal the tile

Using a 3/16-in. trowel, scoop some mastic adhesive out of the tub and put it on the wall (no technique involved here!). Spread the mastic along the centerline, cutting in along the ledger board, vent hood and upper cabinets

3 Tap the tile into the mastic with a wood scrap and a rubber mallet. Stand back, look at the tiles and straighten any crooked ones.

4 Cut tile sheets to the nearest full row to fit around outlets, then fill the gaps with tiles cut on a wet saw.

(Photo 2). Then use broad strokes to fill in the middle. Hold the trowel at a 45-degree angle to the wall to spread the mastic thin—you should be able to see the layout lines where the points of the trowel touch the wall. Have a water bucket and sponge on hand to keep the trowel clean. Whenever the mastic starts to harden on the trowel, wipe it off with the wet sponge.

Place plastic tile spacers on the ledger board and countertop. This leaves a gap so the tiles don't sit directly on the countertop (you'll caulk the gap later).

Align the first tile sheet with the centerline, directly over the spacers. Press it onto the wall with your hand. If the sheet slides around and mastic comes through the joint lines, you're applying the mastic too thick (remove the sheet, scrape off some mastic and retrowel). Scrape out any mastic in the joints with a utility knife.

Eyeball a 1/16-in. joint between sheets of tile (you don't need spacers). After every two or three installed sheets, tap them into the mastic with a board and rubber mallet (Photo 3).

If tiles fall off the sheets, dab a little mastic on the back and stick them right back in place. The sheets

aren't perfectly square, so you may need to move individual tiles to keep joints lined up. Move the tiles with your fingers or by sticking a utility knife blade in the joint and turning the blade. If an entire sheet is crooked, place a grout float over the tile and move the sheet. You'll have about 20 minutes after installing the tile to fine-tune it.

If you're lucky, you can fit the tile sheets under upper cabinets and around outlets by cutting the mesh backing with a utility knife. If not, you'll have to cut the tile with a wet saw. Nippers and grinders cause the slate tiles to shatter or crumble, although you can use these tools on ceramic tile.

Slice the backing to the nearest full row of tile, install the sheet around the outlet or next to the cabinet, then cut tiles with a wet saw to fill the gaps (Photo 4). Cut the tiles while they're attached to the sheet. Individual tiles are too small to cut (the blade can send them flying!).

Let the tile sit for at least 30 minutes, then apply a grout sealer if you're using natural stone (like slate) or unglazed quarry tile. The sealer keeps the grout from sticking to the tile (it's not needed for nonporous tiles

5 Force grout into the joints with a float. Scrape off excess grout by moving the float diagonally across the tile.

6 Rake the grout out of the joints at inside corners and along the bottom with a utility knife so you can fill them with caulk. Keep the dull side of the blade along the countertop.

DULL SIDE

such as ceramic). Pour the sealer on a sponge, then wipe on just enough to dampen the tiles.

Grout and clean the tile

Wait 24 hours after installing the tile to add the grout. Use a premium grout that has a consistent color and resists stain. Since the backsplash will be subject to splatters and stains from cooking and food prep, spend the extra money for a premium grout. You can find it at home centers or tile stores. Use unsanded grout for tile with gaps of 1/8 in. or less, and sanded grout if the gaps are more than 1/8 in.

Mix the grout with water until it reaches mashed potato consistency, then put some on the wall with a grout float. Work the grout into the joints by moving the float diagonally over the tiles (Photo 5). Hold the grout float at a 45-degree angle to the tile. Scrape off excess grout with the float after the joints are filled.

Ten minutes after grouting, wipe the grout off the surface of the tiles with a damp sponge. If the grout pulls out of the joints, wait another 10 minutes for it to harden. Continually rinse the sponge in a bucket of water and

wipe the tiles until they're clean.

These slate tiles have a lot of crevices that retain grout. While most of the grout comes off the tiles with the wet sponge, some won't. Most pro installers leave some grout in slate and other rough-surface tile—it's just part of the deal with some types of natural stone. But if you want the tile completely clean, remove the grout from individual tiles with a toothbrush.

After cleaning the wall, use a utility knife to rake the grout out of the joints along the bottom of the backsplash and in the inside corners (Photo 6). These expansion joints allow the wall to move without cracking the grout.

Two hours after grouting, wipe the haze off the tiles with microfiber cloths. Then caulk the expansion joints with latex caulk. Use a colored caulk that closely matches the grout (available at tile stores).

After seven days, sponge on a grout sealer to protect the grout against stains.

That's it! Now every time your family and friends gather in your kitchen, they'll be impressed with your custom backsplash.

Bathroom
makeover

Y ou don't have to spend thousands of dollars and put up with weeks of construction mess to transform your bathroom. In many cases, you can give your bathroom a fresh, new look by replacing the dated vanity cabinet, sink, faucets and light fixtures. And with a little planning and perseverance, you can get most of the work done in a weekend. In this story, we'll walk you through the steps for this weekend bathroom makeover and show you a few tricks to save you some money and speed up the job.

For more details on vanity tear-out and installation, sink hook-up, sconce wiring and tiling, you can go to familyhandyman.com and search for the topic you're interested in.

WHAT IT TAKES **Time:** 1—2 weekends
Skill level: Intermediate

We were looking for a way to radically change the appearance of this '70s-era bathroom without breaking the bank. And after shopping around, we settled on IKEA cabinets and fixtures. They're modern, moderately priced and easy to install. To spice things up, we splurged a little on the glass tiles. But even at $10 per sq. ft., the tile only added about $270 to the cost. Altogether we spent about $1,300 for this project.

Before you launch into a bath redo like this, make sure the flooring extends under the vanity cabinet. This may take a little detective work. You can usually tell by carefully inspecting the intersection of the floor and cabinet. If there's no flooring under the cabinet, you'll have to either replace the floor or find a new vanity cabinet with the same or larger footprint. If you're lucky, you may find matching flooring to patch in, but this is rare.

Tear out the old stuff

Every bathroom is different, and this phase of the job may be quick and easy or present a few challenges. Start by closing the shutoff valves to the faucet and disconnecting the plumbing under the sink. If the drain parts are the old steel type, don't try to reuse them. You'll save yourself headaches by simply replacing the trap assembly with a modern PVC version. Buy a 1-1/4-in. PVC trap kit at a home center or hardware store. If you have a plastic laminate vanity top, look for screws on the underside and remove them. Cultured marble tops like the one shown here are usually held on by caulk and need to be pried off (Photo 1). If tile surrounds your vanity top, you'll have to remove the tile first.

Next remove the screws that hold the cabinet to the wall and remove the cabinet. Complete the tear-out by removing the mirror or medicine cabinet and light fixtures. Turn off the power to the bathroom light at the main electrical panel and double-check the wires with a voltage sniffer to make sure the power is off before you disconnect the light.

Here's what we did:
- Installed a new IKEA cabinet in place of the old vanity.
- Replaced an old single-bowl vanity top with a modern double-bowl top and faucets from IKEA.
- Added a big mirror to make the room feel spacious.
- Improved the lighting by adding sconces on the sides of the mirror.
- Added style and punch with decorative glass tile.
- Tied it all together with new birch trim to match the cabinet.

1 CULTURED MARBLE TOP

Tear out the vanity. Disconnect the plumbing and pry off the old top. Then remove the vanity cabinet and old medicine cabinet or mirror.

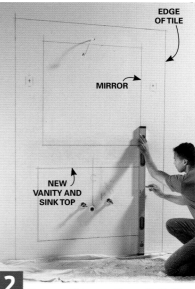

2 EDGE OF TILE — MIRROR — NEW VANITY AND SINK TOP

Draw outlines on the wall. Outline the new fixtures, mirror and tile on the wall. Then decide where the new lights should go and mark these.

Mark the new plan on the wall

Drawing a full-scale plan of the new layout on the wall will save you headaches later (Photo 2). You'll need the dimensions of the vanity cabinet, vanity top, tile and light fixtures. It's best if you have these items on-site to make sure there are no surprises. In addition, it's important to dry-fit the drain parts so you'll know exactly where to position the new vanity cabinet. The IKEA cabinet we used included a custom (and very unusual) drain assembly that required us to center the new cabinet on the existing drain. Traditional vanity cabinets are more forgiving.

After you've determined the

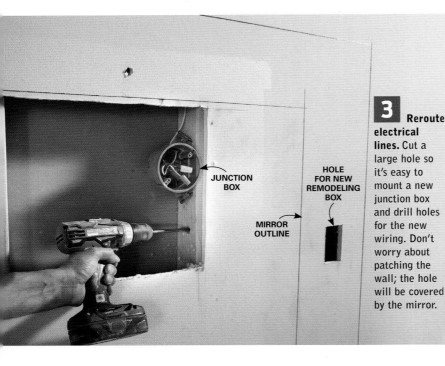

3 **Reroute electrical lines.** Cut a large hole so it's easy to mount a new junction box and drill holes for the new wiring. Don't worry about patching the wall; the hole will be covered by the mirror.

JUNCTION BOX

MIRROR OUTLINE

HOLE FOR NEW REMODELING BOX

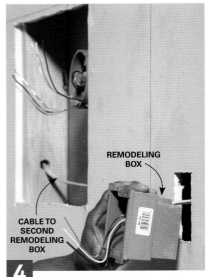

REMODELING BOX

CABLE TO SECOND REMODELING BOX

4 **Mount the new light boxes.** Run a cable from the junction box to the new remodeling boxes. Slide the box into the hole and tighten the screws to clamp it onto the drywall.

BONDERA TILE ADHESIVE

BACK LINER

5 **Apply the tile adhesive.** Line up the edge of the tile adhesive with the tile line. Peel off the back liner as you press the adhesive to the wall.

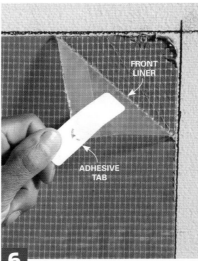

FRONT LINER

ADHESIVE TAB

6 **Peel off the front liner.** Use the sticky tabs included with the tile adhesive to peel off the front liner. Once you get it started, it's easy to peel off the rest.

vanity cabinet location and marked it on the wall, plan the tile layout. Lay a row of tile on the floor to determine the exact width and height of the tiled area and mark this on the wall. Now draw lines to indicate the position of the mirror. Finally mark the location of the new light fixture boxes. Hold the light fixtures up on the wall to determine the best height and make marks. Then center them between the mirror and the tile border. After you double-check all your layout marks, you're ready to move on to the wiring.

Add wiring for the new sconces

Again, every bathroom will be different. Maybe you already have sconces, but need to relocate them for the new mirror position. Keep in mind that the National Electrical Code requires every electrical box to be accessible. In other words, you can't connect wires in a junction box and then cover it with drywall or glue a mirror over it. But luckily it's OK to put a junction box behind a mirror as long as the mirror isn't permanently attached. This allows you some flexibility when adding light fixtures. If the old wires won't reach to the new box location, you can simply add a junction box as we show here and extend new wires from it to the new fixture locations (Photo 3 and 4).

In our case, the wiring was straightforward. There was one cable extending from the switch to the original light fixture. We removed a section of drywall to simplify the installation of the junction box and new wires. Then we chose an electrical box large enough to accommodate the new wires (go to familyhandyman.com and search for "electrical box size" for more information). We nailed the new junction box to the stud and ran the old wires into the box. Then we cut holes for the new remodeling boxes at the fixture locations, drilled holes through the studs and ran new cable from the junction box to each fixture location (Photo 4). We used remodeling boxes to simplify exact placement and avoid extra wall patching.

The adhesive mat is a great time-saver. Just stick it to the wall, press on the tile and you're ready to grout.

Tile the walls

It's easier to tile before you install the vanity cabinet because you don't have to cut the tile to fit around it. You can save money on tile by omitting it behind the vanity cabinet and mirror. Just extend the tile a few inches beyond the outlines of the mirror and cabinet. Also, you don't have to cut tile to fit tightly to the electrical boxes as long as the light fixture will cover the missing tiles.

Rather than spread thin-set mortar on the wall to adhere the tile, we installed a sticky tile adhesive mat (Bondera is one brand) (Photos 5 and 6). Tile adhesive has a few advantages over thin-set, especially for installation of glass mosaic tile like ours. First, you can grout right away. You don't have to wait for the thin-set to set up. And you don't have to worry about thin-set oozing out from behind the tile and into the grout spaces.

Tile adhesive isn't perfect, though. First, it's way more expensive than thin-set. Also, repositioning the sheets of tile was a little tricky. They won't slide like they do on thin-set. You have to place them gingerly onto the mat and not embed them firmly until you're sure they're properly aligned. You can pull off the sheet of tile and reposition it if you haven't pressed too hard. Follow the instructions included with the adhesive, or go to the manufacturer's web site for an installation video and more instructions.

If you're leaving tile out like we did, the trick is to make sure the tile meets up accurately as you surround the blank space. Run tile up one side to just above the cabinet space and across the bottom, making sure the side column is perfectly plumb (follow your layout line) and the bottom row is perfectly

BONDERA TILE ADHESIVE
GLASS MOSAIC TILE SHEET

7 **Install the tile.** Position the tile carefully and press it just hard enough to hold it in place. When you're sure the tile is straight and the joints line up, tamp the tile with a grout float to adhere it.

8 **Grout the tile.** Press grout into the joints with a grout float. Sweep the float in diagonal strokes until the joints are completely filled. Then scrape off the excess grout with the edge of the float.

Tile adhesive mat: A new way to set tile

To install the glass mosaics for this project, we replaced the traditional thin-set mortar tile adhesive with a tile adhesive mat. It's basically a mat that's sticky on both sides, allowing you to stick it to the wall like wallpaper, and then stick tiles to the face. Tile adhesive mats are available at home centers and online for about $40 for a 12-in.-wide x 10-ft.-long roll. The main advantages over thin-set are that you can grout right away and that you don't have to worry about it oozing into the grout joints. It's not perfect, though. Whereas thin-set can take up some wall irregularities, tile adhesive mat isn't forgiving. If your wall is wavy, your tile will be too. And you can't slide the tile around to reposition it. You can nudge it a little, but for major adjustments you'll have to pull off the tile and try again.

Here's what Dean, our tile guru, has to say:

"I'm impressed! The tile really sticks to this stuff. It would be great for my kitchen backsplash jobs. I'd save a trip back and the customer would be happy to have me out of the kitchen a day sooner."

level. Then extend lines from these two points with a level. Remember, don't press too hard on the tile until you're sure it's all lined up correctly (Photo 7). When the tile is lined up

perfectly, embed it in the mat by tamping on it with a grout float. As soon as you're done tiling, you can mix up some grout and fill the grout spaces (Photo 8).

Mix the grout to toothpaste consistency and let it sit for 15 minutes. Remix it and add a tiny dash of water if it got too thick. Go to familyhandyman.com and type "grout" into the search box for more grouting tips and instructions.

Mount the vanity cabinet and top

IKEA cabinets require assembly but are easy to put together. After assembling the cabinet, mount it on the wall using temporary blocks to hold it up. If you don't have studs at the mounting bracket location, use toggle bolts. Regardless of what type of vanity cabinet you're installing, first locate the studs. Then drive 3-in. washer head screws through the cabinet hanging rail into the studs to hold it in place (Photo 9).

Next mount the faucets to the sink top and assemble the drain parts and faucet connections. If you're replacing a single faucet with two faucets, you can connect them both to the existing shutoff valves by adding a "tee" as shown in Photo 10. These IKEA faucets included proprietary supply tubes with 1/2-in. pipe thread fittings on the end. Your faucets may be different. Take the faucet and any included tubes with you to the home center or hardware store so you can assemble them in the store to find the right parts.

After you've mounted the faucets and assembled the drain parts, you're ready to install the sink. Spread a thin bead of silicone caulk on the top edge of the cabinet and carefully lower the sink top onto it. Let the caulk set up for a few hours before you connect the plumbing to make sure the sink doesn't get jostled out of position. Complete the job by marking and cutting the PVC tailpiece (Photo 11) and connecting the supply lines. Turn on the water and check for leaks.

Add the finishing touches

Now you're on the home stretch. In our bathroom, we repainted the walls and replaced the old moldings with strips of flat birch to match the new cabinet. Photo 12 shows how to drill holes in the glass tile for the mirror mounting clips. The mirror mounts we found at the home center included a pair of spring-loaded clips for the top and fixed clips for the bottom. Measure your mirror and mark the clip positions on the tiles with a permanent

9 **Hang the cabinet.** Support the cabinet on temporary stands. Then drive screws through the hanging rail into the studs to secure the cabinet.

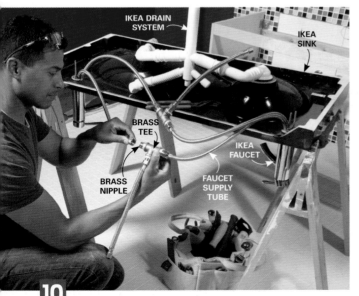

10 **Mount the faucets.** Follow the faucet instructions to mount the faucets to the sink. Installing the faucets and drain plumbing is easier if you do it before installing the sink on the cabinet.

11 **Connect the plumbing.** Mark the tailpiece so that it will extend into the trap a few inches when it's cut off. Cut it off with a hacksaw. Remove the trap. Slip it over the tailpiece and reconnect it. Connect the supply tubes to the shutoff valves. Turn on the water and check for leaks.

12 **Drill mirror clip holes.** Keep the glass bit cool by spraying water on it as you drill. Run the drill at slow to medium speed. Let up on the pressure when you're almost through the tile.

MIRROR CLIP

PLASTIC ANCHOR

13 **Install the mirror clips.** Tap a plastic hollow-wall anchor into the hole and screw the clip into the anchor. If the hole landed over a stud, you don't need the anchor.

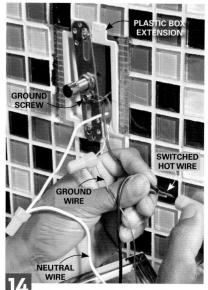

PLASTIC BOX EXTENSION

GROUND SCREW

SWITCHED HOT WIRE

GROUND WIRE

NEUTRAL WIRE

14 **Wire the light fixtures.** Slip a box extension into the electrical box if the tile is more than 1/4 in. thick. Then mount the fixture strap to the box and connect the wires.

TIP:
The trick to drilling a hole in glass tile is to go slow and keep the glass bit wet.

1/4" GLASS BIT

marker. The top clips have to be mounted about 3/8 in. low to allow the spring clip to function properly. Then use a 1/4-in. glass bit, available at home centers and hardware stores, to drill the holes (Photo 12). The key is to go slowly and keep the bit and tile wet to avoid overheating, which would crack the tile and ruin the bit. Tap a plastic anchor into the holes and attach the clips with pan head screws. Install the mirror by putting the top edge into the clips and lifting it up. Then let it drop down into the lower clips.

Finish by mounting the light fixtures. Make sure the power is turned off. Then strip the ends of the wires about 1/2 in. (read the instructions on the wire connector package for the exact amount). Electrical boxes can be recessed up to 1/4 in. in noncombustible materials like tile, but since our tile was just over 1/4 in. thick, we added a box extension set flush to the tile surface before attaching the fixture strap with

15 **Finish up.** Hang the mirror, paint the walls and mount the light fixtures. We installed new trim to match the cabinet.

the mounting screws (Photo 14). Wrap the bare copper ground wire three-quarters of the way around the grounding screw on the fixture strap and tighten the screw. Then extend the remainder of the bare

ground wire to the ground wire on the fixture and connect them with a wire connector. Complete the wiring by connecting the white neutral wires together and the switched hot wires together.

Weekend wainscoting

Traditional elegance, home-center materials

For this room, we wanted a frame-and-panel wainscoting that matched the doors and traditional trim. Well, we wanted it until we saw the price tag. That's when we came up with a design that we could make quickly and cheaply, using stock material.

Here's the basic idea. The frame is made from 1/2-in. MDF; this thickness makes a better transition where the wainscoting meets the door or window trim. Instead of a traditional panel, the frame has rectangular openings, through which you see the wall. This gives some interesting options: another paint color (our choice), a decorative paint texture like rag-rolling, or even wallpaper. Moldings frame the openings and also form the cap along the top edge.

Wainscoting has to be fit to the length of your walls, so we can't give you complete dimensions. You'll have to adjust the width of the openings so they're the same all along the wall. The simplest way is to figure out how many openings fit along the wall. Then take the leftover and spread it out between them. Draw your proposed wainscoting on the wall to check your layout.

Once you have a layout that works, cut your MDF and moldings. Prime all the parts, then nail the MDF to the wall. Attach to studs when possible, but if it's not, use a little construction adhesive and nail at an angle to give some grip. Attach all the moldings, fill the nail holes and then paint. Bob's your uncle!

Figure A
Upper rail construction

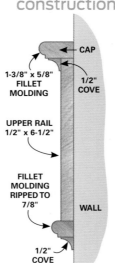

CAP

1-3/8" x 5/8" FILLET MOLDING

1/2" COVE

UPPER RAIL 1/2" x 6-1/2"

FILLET MOLDING RIPPED TO 7/8"

WALL

1/2" COVE

Figure B
Wainscoting construction

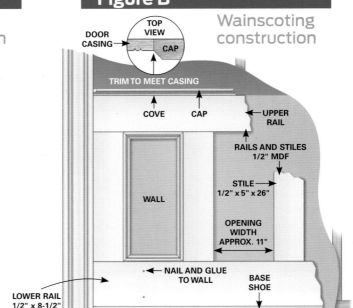

TOP VIEW

DOOR CASING

CAP

TRIM TO MEET CASING

COVE   CAP

UPPER RAIL

RAILS AND STILES 1/2" MDF

WALL

STILE 1/2" x 5" x 26"

OPENING WIDTH APPROX. 11"

NAIL AND GLUE TO WALL

BASE SHOE

LOWER RAIL 1/2" x 8-1/2"

WHAT IT TAKES

Time: 1 weekend
Skill level: Beginner

Transform a room with painted rectangles

For less than $100, you can transform a room in a single weekend. All it takes is some paint, glaze and masking tape.

The techniques for masking and glazing are easy to learn and don't require any special skills. However, you will need a good bit of patience since the finish entails multiple layers of glaze and careful applications of masking tape. You only need to paint one wall to achieve a dramatic effect. You could complete a wall in a day, but it's better to set aside a weekend to allow plenty of drying time between coats of glaze.

The first step is to paint the wall with the base coat color. For this you'll need typical painting supplies like a stepladder, drop cloth, paintbrush and roller.

Recipe for rectangles

(Editor's Note: Paint color names and numbers change, but use this recipe as a guide for adding glaze.)

Base coat color: Benjamin Moore Semolina 2155-40, eggshell.

First set of rectangles: One part Benjamin Moore Dash of Curry 2159-10 thinned with 3 parts Benjamin Moore Latex Glaze Extender Clear 408.

Second set of rectangles: One part Modern Masters Tequila Gold ME661 thinned with two parts Glaze Extender.

Third set of rectangles: One part Modern Masters Gold Rush ME658 thinned with two parts Glaze Extender.

Fourth layer of rectangles: One part Modern Masters Flash Copper ME656 thinned with one part Glaze Extender.

Random rectangles

Four layers of glazed boxes overlap to create this contemporary design. Golden hues are used here, but you could produce the same effect using different colors. In general, use a darker or more opaque color for the first layer of boxes, and lighten the color and increase the transparency for each of the three succeeding layers. Where layers overlap, new shades and colors will appear. That's why it's essential to create a sample board before you start.

Latex paint thinned with glaze was used for the first layer, and thinned semi-opaque metallic finishes were used for the next two layers. Before you commit to applying the finish to the wall, choose your colors and mix the glazes. Then make a sample board by painting a piece of drywall, hardboard or MDF (medium-density fiberboard) and applying the glaze. Overlap sections of glaze on the board to see the effect. Of course, if you like the way this wall looks, just copy the recipe shown in the box above. When you're happy with the choice of colors, you can start on the wall.

Choosing the size and position of the boxes may seem daunting, but don't worry. The wall will look better with each layer you apply. Buy a watercolor pencil at an art supply store in a color that matches your color scheme and use it to mark the walls. The watercolor lines will disappear as you apply the glaze to the boxes. Square and rectangular boxes that ranged in size from a 34 x 14-in. rectangle to a 48-in. square were used here. Photos 1 – 3 show the process. Draw the fourth layer of boxes to enclose any base coat color that hasn't been covered by previous layers.

Tape off a series of boxes. Then, using the following steps, you'll spread a thin layer of glaze within the taped-off boxes to create a cloudy effect. Wet the sponges and wring them out before starting. Then use one sponge to spread a few 6-in.-long swaths of glaze on a small section of a box. "Pounce" the flat side of a second dampened sponge onto the glaze to spread it out. Rinse the pouncing sponge in clean water occasionally to get rid of built-up glaze. Work quickly across the box so that you never have to overlap onto an area of glaze that's already dry. Complete all the boxes with the first glaze color and let the glaze dry at least a couple of hours before starting on the next layer.

Draw another set of boxes on the wall that overlaps the first set and repeat the glazing process. Repeat these steps for the third layer. Complete the wall by covering any unglazed base coat with the fourth layer of glazed rectangles.

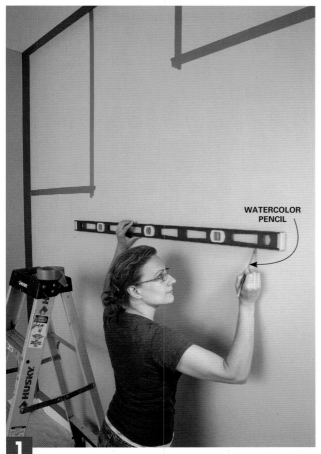

1 Mark rectangles on the wall using a level and a watercolor pencil. Then frame the rectangles with masking tape.

WATERCOLOR PENCIL

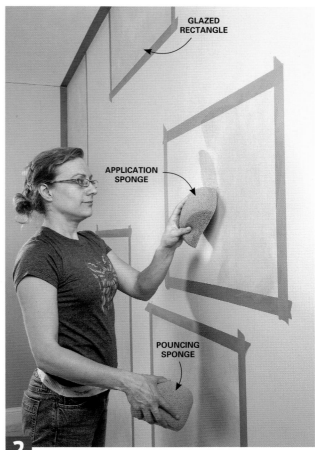

GLAZED RECTANGLE

APPLICATION SPONGE

POUNCING SPONGE

2 Spread random 6-in. swaths of glaze with the end of a sponge. Pounce with the second sponge to spread the glaze.

SECOND LAYER OF GLAZE

3 Add a second, third and fourth layer of overlapping boxes, using a lighter-colored glaze for each layer. Let the glaze dry at least two hours between layers.

Corner technique

Finishing right up to an inside corner with a sponge is difficult. You'll get uneven coverage or a buildup of glaze that looks bad. A better technique is to finish within a few inches of the corner with the sponge. Then, while the finish is still wet, use a dry brush in a pouncing motion to work the glaze into the corner.

Replace your trim with a classic look

This Old World elegance is actually easier than standard trim

This traditional trim style may look like it requires old-school carpentry skills, but the truth is, it's easier to install than contemporary trim. Modern trim—four pieces of casing that "picture frame" a door or window—requires wide miter cuts, which look sloppy if they're not perfect. Traditional trim is more forgiving. While it also requires miter cuts, they're shorter and less visible. And the most prominent joints are assembled with simple square cuts.

If you're nervous about installing the mitered crown molding that tops off the trim, check out "Make Your Own Moldings" on p. 75 where we show you how to make a simple router-shaped version that doesn't require any miters. We'll walk you through the steps and give you some tips and pointers for cutting and installing the moldings to create this classic trim style.

Getting started

The first step in any trim job is to prepare the jambs for trim. If you're replacing trim, pry it off and remove the nails from the jamb. Then scrape or sand the face of the jamb to smooth out any paint or finish that's built up. Finally, mark the reveal on the jambs to show where the edge of the trim goes (Photo 1, inset). A combination square set to 1/4 in. works great for marking the reveals. But you can also use a compass to scribe the marks, or simply measure and mark the reveals.

If possible, set up your miter saw in the room where you're installing the trim. Having the saw nearby will save you a ton of time. I like to rough-cut the casing and other moldings to length, allowing a few extra inches, and label them to make sure I have all the material I need and won't accidentally cut the wrong piece.

For tips on buying or making the moldings you'll need, see p. 75.

Mark, don't measure

With the moldings and other parts cut to rough length, and the reveals marked on the jambs, the fastest and most accurate method for marking the trim for cutting is to simply hold the molding in place and mark it (Photo 1). It's foolproof. You don't have to measure, do math or remember any numbers.

Install the window casings, stool and apron

The order of trim installation for windows varies a little depending on whether you're working on old double-hung windows or newer-style windows. On older double-hung windows, the stool rests on the angled sill and butts into the lower sash (check out Figure A if you're not sure what a stool is). You have to notch the new stool to fit, and nail it to the windowsill before you install the side casings. But on newer windows like the one shown here, the stool isn't notched and doesn't rest on the sill, so it's a little trickier to nail. An easy way to attach this type of stool is to install the side casings first, and then nail the stool to them (Photo 2).

The stool should protrude past the casings by about an inch (Photo 2). To find the length of the stool, make a mark 1 in. beyond the casing on both sides. Then hold the stool up and transfer the marks. After the stool material is cut to length, round the edges and ends. Or if you want a little fancier stool, rout the edges with a more decorative bit. You can even buy a special stool-shaping bit, but you may have to order it.

With the side casings and stool in place, the next step is to install the apron under the stool. Start by cutting a 45-degree miter on each end. Mark for the long point of the miters by resting the apron on the stool and making marks where the outside edges of the casings intersect the apron material. Snug the mitered apron against the bottom of the stool and nail it to the framing under

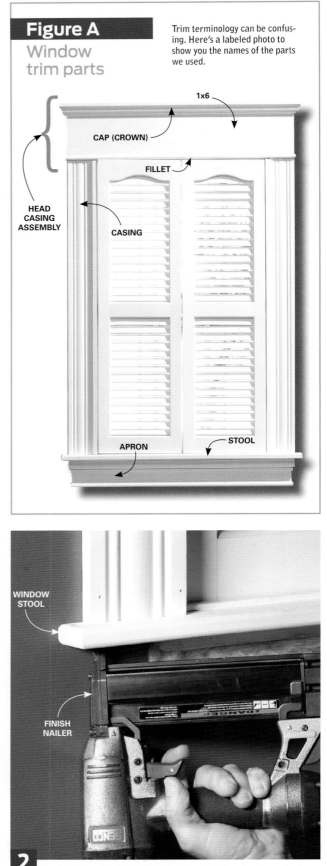

Figure A
Window trim parts

Trim terminology can be confusing. Here's a labeled photo to show you the names of the parts we used.

1x6

CAP (CROWN)

FILLET

HEAD CASING ASSEMBLY

CASING

APRON

STOOL

1 **Mark the side casing.** Cut one end of the casing square. Line up the cut end with the pencil mark indicating the 1/4-in. reveal and mark the opposite end for cutting. Cut and install both side casings, keeping them aligned with the reveal marks.

TOP REVEAL MARK

1/4"

BOTTOM REVEAL MARK

BOTTOM REVEAL MARK

2 **Install the stool.** Cut the stool so that it extends an inch past the casing on both ends. Then round the edges with a router or by sanding. Nail the stool to the side casings.

WINDOW STOOL

FINISH NAILER

Traditional molding

Tips for choosing, buying and making your own

Shopping for trim

We found the wide casing and base blocks at the home center, along with the fancy casing we used as an apron. We had to go to the local lumberyard for the 2-1/4-in. crown molding. If your local home center or lumberyard doesn't have what you want in stock, ask to see a molding book or chart that shows what styles are available to order. The Internet is also a good place to search for traditional moldings. Start with "molding and millwork."

Make your own moldings

You don't have to buy moldings. With a little ingenuity and a few standard router bits, you can make your own. Figure B shows an example of a cap molding for a head casing that we made by stacking two pieces of 3/4-in. oak. Shaping the edges of wood strips with a router and stacking them to make bigger moldings is a great technique for making your own moldings.

You can make moldings with a hand-held router, but it's a lot easier and faster to mount your router in a router table. The Ryobi router table shown here works well, but there are plenty of other options. For plans to make your own, go to familyhandyman.com and search for "router table."

The photo at right shows how to use featherboards for safer and more accurate routing. You can make your own featherboards, or buy plastic ones like these for about $10 to $20 each.

The ends of the boards shown in Figure B are routed. This method eliminates the need for mitered returns, but it does expose end grain and means you have to cut the parts to length before you shape them. To rout the end of boards, use a shop-made push block like the one shown at the top of the page. It serves two functions. First, it allows you to hold the board square to the fence. And second, the push block prevents splintering by providing a backer behind the board you're routing.

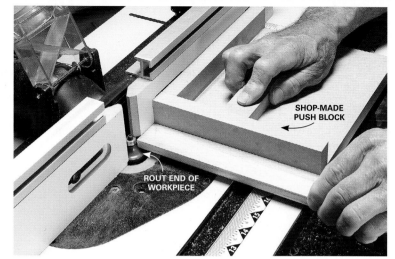

Build a simple push block to rout ends. Hold the board square to the fence and prevent tear-out with a shop-made push block like this.

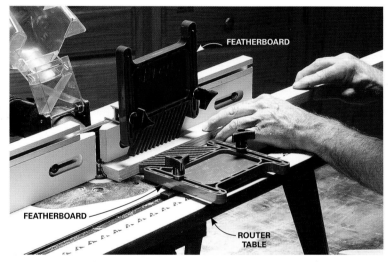

Hold the wood with featherboards. When you're making moldings with a router table, use featherboards to hold the wood tight to the fence and table. Set the featherboards to apply light pressure.

Figure B
Router-shaped cap molding

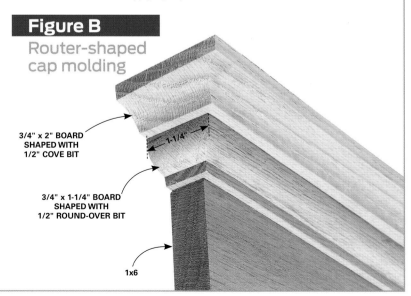

3/4" x 2" BOARD SHAPED WITH 1/2" COVE BIT

1-1/4"

3/4" x 1-1/4" BOARD SHAPED WITH 1/2" ROUND-OVER BIT

1x6

3 **Cut the mitered apron returns.** Set the miter saw to 45 degrees and cut a return from the apron molding. Use a sacrificial board to prevent the small cutoff from flying through the gap in the fence. Set the miter saw to the opposite angle to cut the other return from the opposite end of the molding.

the window. Then cut returns and glue them in (Photos 3 and 4).

Photo 3 shows how to use a sacrificial piece of wood behind the apron material. Any flat scrap of wood will work. This sacrificial backer board prevents the skinny piece of molding you're cutting off from getting caught by the blade and flung through the gap in the fence. Don't attach the sacrificial board to the saw. Just hold it in place along with the molding you're cutting. Then reposition it with each new cut so you're always making a fresh cut through the sacrificial board.

Build the head casing assembly

The final step for both the door and the window trim is building and installing the head casing assembly. It's made up of three parts: the fillet, a 1x6 and the cap molding. Traditionally this cap molding was solid, but since a solid molding this large is hard to come by, we substituted 2-1/4-in. crown molding. If you have a router and want to avoid using crown molding, check out Figure B on p. 75 for an attractive alternative.

Start by setting the 1x6 on top of the side casings and marking it at the outside edge of each casing. Cut the 1x6 to length. Then cut the fillet 3/4 in. longer than the 1x6. Round over the edges and ends of the fillet to make a bullnose shape using a router and 1/4-in. round-over bit. Nail the fillet to the bottom of the 1x6.

Finish the head casing by wrapping the front and sides of the 1x6 with crown molding. Photos 5 – 8 show how. Make a jig (Photo 6 and Figure C) to hold the crown molding at the correct angle while you cut it. Remember to set the crown molding upside down in the jig. Mark

4 **Finish the apron.** Glue in the returns to complete the apron. Avoid nailing problems by letting the glue do the work. Just hold the return in place for 60 seconds while the glue grabs.

5 **Mark the crown molding for the end return.** Hold a piece of crown molding against the 1x6 you'll be using for the head casing and mark it for cutting.

6 **Build a crown-molding jig.** Build a simple jig to hold the crown molding at the correct angle while you cut it. Position the molding upside down and set the saw to 45 degrees. Avoid cutting all the way through the jig.

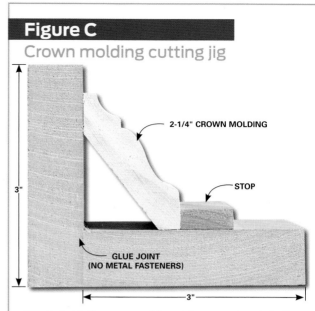

2-1/4" CROWN MOLDING

STOP

3"

GLUE JOINT (NO METAL FASTENERS)

3"

This jig holds the crown molding at the correct angle in the miter saw, so it's easy to make accurate miters every time. Glue two strips of scrap wood together at a right angle. Then set the crown molding upside down in the jig and mark the position of the stop. Glue the stop to the bottom and you're ready to cut some moldings.

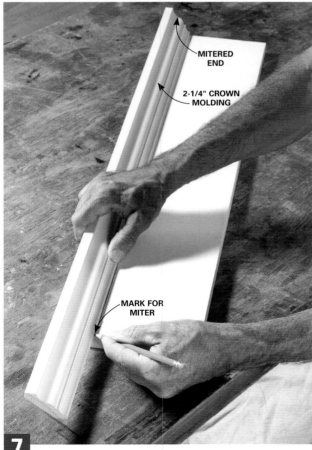

MITERED END

2-1/4" CROWN MOLDING

MARK FOR MITER

7 **Mark the front crown molding.** Cut a miter on one end of the front crown molding. Line up the cut with one end of the head casing and mark the opposite end for cutting. Set the molding in your jig and cut the opposite miter.

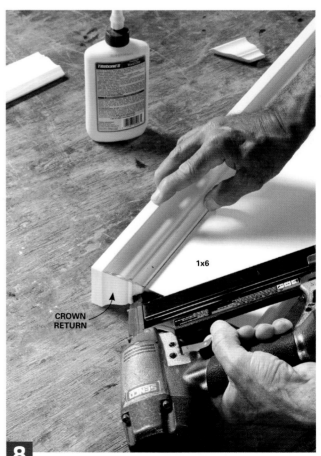

1x6

CROWN RETURN

8 **Attach the molding to the head casing.** Nail the crown molding to the 1x6. Then glue and nail in the end returns. Nail the fillet to the bottom of the 1x6 to complete the head casing assembly.

and cut the short pieces of crown molding (Photos 5 and 6). Then cut a miter on one end of the long front piece and hold it in place on the 1x6 to mark the opposite end for the miter (Photo 7). Cut the second miter on the front piece.

Check the fit by holding the short mitered ends in place against the front crown molding. If the miters are tight and everything fits, complete the head casing by nailing the crown molding to the 1x6 (Photo 8). Complete the window trim by nailing the head casing assembly to the framing above the window (Photo 9).

Finishing up

If you're installing painted moldings like ours, go to family-handyman.com and enter "paint trim" in the search box for tips on how to finish your moldings with a flawless coat of paint. You can also find tips for staining and finishing wood by entering "stain trim" in the search box.

9 **Finish the window trim.** Set the head casing on the side casings, making sure the fillet overhangs evenly on both ends. Then nail it to the wall framing.

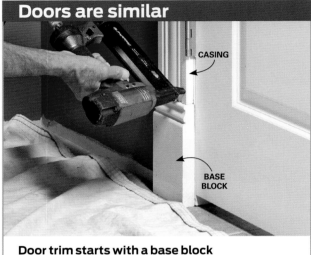

Doors are similar

Door trim starts with a base block at the bottom

Trimming a door is just like trimming a window, except you start out with base blocks at the floor, as shown above. The base blocks should be about 3/8 in. wider than the casings. Trim them if necessary. The height of the base blocks should be about 1 in. greater than the height of the baseboard you're planning to install.

Buying nail guns

If you can afford it, buy both a 15-gauge finish nailer and an 18-gauge brad nailer. The two guns make a winning combination. The 15-gauge nails, ranging in length from about 1-1/4 in. to 2-1/2 in., are strong enough to secure door jambs and other heavy trim materials. Plus, the angled nose on most 15-gauge nailers allows you to nail in corners and drive toenails more easily.

Fifteen-gauge nails are too thick for many fine nailing tasks. And this is where the 18-gauge brad nailer excels. They shoot very skinny 5/8-in. to 1 1/2-in.-long, 18-gauge brads. These are perfect for nailing miters, nailing the skinny section of door or window casing to the jamb and other nailing jobs where a larger nail would split the wood or protrude through the other side of the material. Good-quality brad nailers are available for less than $100.

Having both guns connected to your compressor with separate hoses means you can nail the inside and outside edge of casings without having to change nails. And you'll always have just the right size nail for the job at hand.

If you don't do enough trim work to justify the expense of two nailers, a 16-gauge nail gun is a good choice. The 16-gauge nails are a bit skinnier and not quite as strong as 15-gauge nails. But they're less likely to split thin pieces of wood. Most 16-gauge nail guns will shoot nails ranging from 1 in. to 2-1/4 in. There are also a few 18-gauge brad nailers that can shoot nails up to 2-1/4 in., but the nails are not strong enough for heavy work like door jambs.

Hide the nail heads

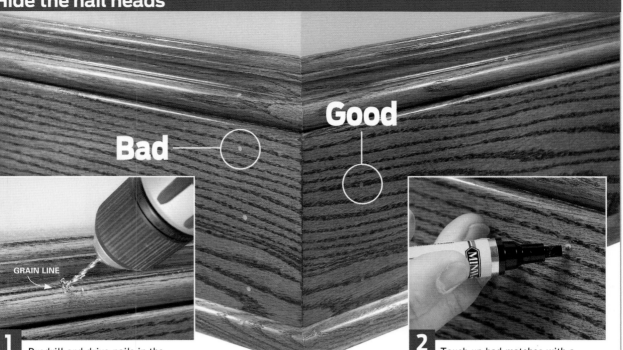

Bad

Good

GRAIN LINE

1 Predrill and drive nails in the darker grain lines when possible. Holes there are much easier to hide.

2 Touch up bad matches with a colored felt-tip pen. Or drill out the old putty and refill.

If you want your trim work to have a rustic, distressed look, go ahead and make the nail holes stand out. But if you're seeking a smooth, furniture-like finish, you have to make those nail holes disappear. Hiding nail holes takes a little more time and patience, but you'll get the fine, flawless appearance you want.

Begin by staining and sealing the trim before you put it up. Then buy colored putties to closely match the stain colors on the wood (Photo 3). (The other option, filling the holes with stainable filler before staining, is tricky unless you have a lot of experience.) Prestaining also makes the darker grain lines of the wood stand out. Position your nails there for the least visibility.

Buy several putty colors and mix them to match the wood color. Wood tone is rarely uniform, even when the wood is stained, so you can't rely on only one color to fill every hole (Photo 3). Fine-tune your blends, and set your test piece alongside the trim to check the visibility of the nail holes under real light conditions. Lighting can significantly affect whether the filler blends or stands out.

Keep in mind that you can correct past mistakes or fix a situation where the wood has darkened after a year or two (with cherry, for example). Simply buy wood-tone felt-tip pens and touch up the filler (Photo 2). Or lightly drill out the most unsightly old filler holes with a small drill bit and refill them. Minwax is one common brand of colored putties and touch-up pens available at most hardware stores and home centers.

COLORED PUTTY

3 Blend putty colors to more closely match the finished wood colors. One color won't do it all.

TEST PIECE

Install a new interior door

Hanging a door correctly is one of the most satisfying jobs in the home improvement world, but it's often the most challenging. Unless it's installed correctly, your door can have uneven gaps along the jamb, or it can bind or not even latch.

Here you'll learn foolproof tips and techniques that'll give you great results every time. All you need are simple carpentry tools and some basic home improvement skills and tools to easily master the techniques. Allow about an hour and a half for your first door, and once you get the hang of it, your next door will go in twice as fast.

WHAT IT TAKES **Time:** 1 hour per door
Skill level: Intermediate

When you buy your door, pick up a package of wood shims and 4d, 6d and 8d finish nails. Also get a straight 7-ft. 2x4 and cut another 2x4 the width of your opening (Photo 1). Make sure that they are both straight as you sight down the edge. Since installing trim is part of the door installation, purchase some matching door trim and be sure you've got a miter saw to cut it. You'll also need to pick up a lockset for the door.

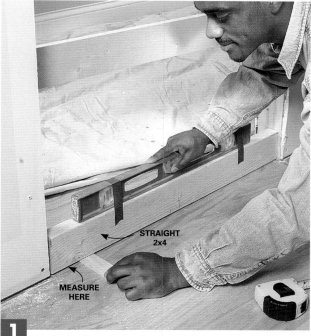

1 Check the floor for level and the jambs for plumb. Measure the exact amount the floor is off level. The opposite jamb must be cut by this much to level the door in the opening.

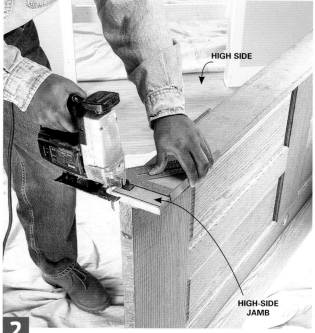

2 Mark and cut the jamb on the high side with your saw (remove any packaging strips at the bottom of the jambs). If you cut more than 1/4 in. from the jamb, you may need to trim the bottom of the door so it conforms to the floor slope.

Check your rough opening carefully before starting

Here the focus is on installing standard prehung doors. These have a door jamb that's 4-9/16 in. wide and are made to fit into a 2x4 wall that's 4-1/2 in. thick. This gives just enough of a fudge factor to have the jamb a bit proud of (raised above) the wall surface on each side and to make up for any irregularities in the trimmer studs of the walls. Most openings will be about 82 in. high for standard doors, so that's what is shown here.

Before you order your door, check the width of your opening. It should be 2 to 2-1/2 in. wider than the door. This extra space gives you room to fit the jambs and the shims into the opening to hang the door. If your rough opening is 32 in., get a 30-in. prehung door. Also check the vertical sides of the rough opening to make sure they're reasonably plumb. Openings that have a trimmer stud out of plumb more than 3/8 in. from top to bottom will make it nearly impossible to install the door. It would be somewhat like trying to put a rectangle into a parallelogram. Small variations from plumb are quite common, however. Checking both sides and getting familiar with any problems with the opening will give you an idea of how much and where to shim the jambs later.

> **TIP:**
> If you're setting your door into adjoining rooms that'll be carpeted later, you can hold both jamb sides 3/8 in. above the floor and avoid having to trim your doors.

3 Nail temporary cleats to the wall opposite the door opening to act as stops for the door frame. To ensure the jambs are centered in the wall, shim them away from the drywall slightly with a stack of three note cards as shown.

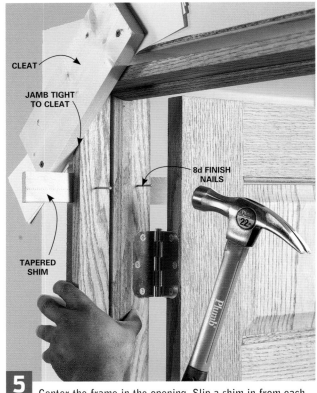

4 Push the door and frame into the opening. Open the door and shim the bottom edge of the open door to keep the frame tight against the stops on the other side.

CLEAT

SHIMS

CLEAT

JAMB TIGHT TO CLEAT

8d FINISH NAILS

TAPERED SHIM

5 Center the frame in the opening. Slip a shim in from each side of the jamb (make sure the frame is pushed against the cleats) and nail the top sides of the door frame into the trimmer studs. The jamb should be perpendicular to your temporary cleats. Be careful not to twist the jamb as you nail it.

DOOR JAMB SHIMMED AND NAILED AT TOP

SHIM

6 Shim the bottom of the door jamb up about 4 in. from the floor on the hinge side, making sure the hinge side is exactly plumb, and then nail it. Tape your level to a straight 2x4 as shown. Next, shim the center area of the jamb to straighten it and then nail it. Check the whole length with your straightedge.

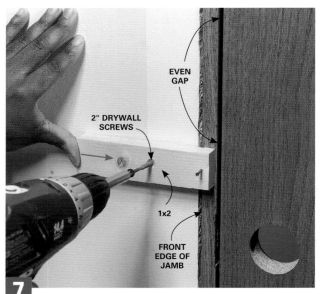

EVEN GAP

2" DRYWALL SCREWS

1x2

FRONT EDGE OF JAMB

7 Tack a 4-in. 1x2 to the front edge of the jamb with a 4d finish nail. Set up an even 3/16-in. gap between the door and the strike-side jamb. Then screw the block to the studs to hold the jamb in this position.

TIP:

Check the length of your prehung door jambs. They may be longer than you need. You may have to trim both sides to minimize the space under the door. In most cases, the door should clear the floor by 1/2 in.

SHIM

8d FINISH NAILS

8 Shim and nail the strike side near the strike plate and then near the floor.

Most installation problems occur because the floor isn't level under the doorway. If the floor slopes slightly and the jamb isn't trimmed to compensate, your latch won't line up. You must check the floor with an accurate level as shown in Photo 1.

How do you fit the jamb to floors of different heights?

Cut a 1-ft.-long strip of 1/4-in. plywood the same width as your door jamb. Drop it to the high side of the floor, tack it in place, set your scribe and mark the contour of the floor onto the plywood. Remove the plywood, cut the shape with a jigsaw and transfer the shape to the bottom of the jamb. Cut along your mark with a jigsaw. Do this for each side of the door. If your transition is more than 1/2 in., you may need to trim the bottom of the door as well.

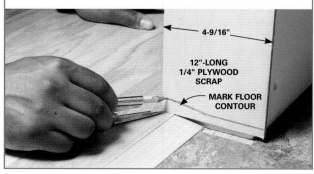

4-9/16"

12"-LONG 1/4" PLYWOOD SCRAP

MARK FLOOR CONTOUR

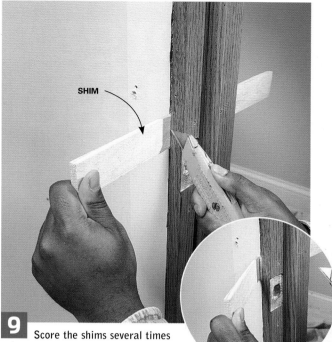

SHIM

9 Score the shims several times with a sharp blade and then snap them off to make way for the trim.

6d FINISH NAIL

4d FINISH NAIL

10 Nail the trim to the door frame with No. 4 finish nails. Nail the trim to the framing with No. 6 finish nails.

TIP:
An accurate level is crucial for a good installation. Check it by laying it on a flat surface. Memorize the bubble's position. Then flip the level end for end and check the bubble. If the bubble doesn't settle in the exact spot, find an accurate level.

An organized closet

Endless combinations!

Here's the key to this whole system: The large box is twice as tall as the small box, and the height of each box is equal to twice its width. That means you can combine them in dozens of different configurations. For more versatility, you can drill holes and add adjustable shelf supports to any of the boxes.

WHAT IT TAKES

Time: 1 weekend
Skill level: Beginner

These easy-to-build boxes suit any situation. They're easy to build, easy to customize and a money-saver besides.

Money, materials and tools

Materials for the boxes shown cost about $250, with an additional $40 to $50 on closet hardware. The 3/4-in. birch plywood is strong and thick enough to accept screws. It also finishes well, and the simple grain and warm color look good with just about any décor.

A 4 x 8-ft. sheet costs $45 to $50. Here's a rule of thumb for estimating the plywood you'll need: One sheet will get you two large boxes or four small boxes, plus some leftover parts. If you don't have a pickup, have the plywood ripped into roughly 16-in.-wide pieces at the home center and then rip it to 15 in. at home.

Before you start cutting up box parts, check the thickness of your plywood. Most "3/4-in." plywood is actually 23/32 in. thick, and the measurements given on p. 86 are based on that. If your plywood is thicker or thinner, you'll have to adjust your box part sizes. The measurements given also account for the typical thickness of iron-on edge band.

A simple jig for perfect crosscuts

To make this closet system work, you need to cut lots of box parts to exact, identical lengths. This plywood jig makes that foolproof. Build the jig and you'll find lots of other uses for it. You can use it to build bookcases, cabinets or shelves.

If your saw is out of whack, you won't get accurate cuts. So do a quick inspection: Measure from the front and back of the blade to the edge of the saw's shoe to make sure the blade runs parallel to the shoe. Then grab a square and make sure the blade is set at 90 degrees to the shoe. Install a 40-tooth carbide blade for clean cuts.

Take your time when you build and install the carriage assembly. First, screw the guide to the carriage. Then run your saw along the guide; that will trim the carriage to suit your saw. When you mount the carriage on the rails, use a framing square to make sure the carriage is perfectly perpendicular to the rails. You can add a stick-on measuring tape to your jig. One last note: Be sure to set the saw depth so it just grazes the jig's base. If you set the saw too deep, you'll cut your new jig in half.

1 Cut a bunch of box parts. This simple jig lets you churn out precise, identical box parts fast. Raise the stop block on a 1/4-in. spacer so dust buildup doesn't throw off the accuracy.

SPACER

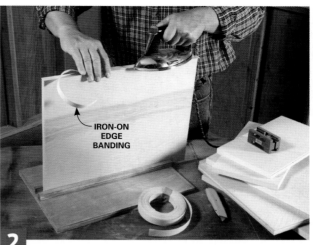

IRON-ON EDGE BANDING

2 Edge-band the parts. Cover the visible edges with iron-on edge band. Band only the front edges of the short parts (B, E). On the long parts (A, D), band three edges.

SUPPORT BOARD

3 Cut the biscuit slots. Clamp a support board flush with the edge to keep the biscuit joiner from rocking as you cut.

Band, biscuit and assemble

If you haven't edge-banded plywood before (Photo 2), don't be intimidated; it's a skill you can master in a few minutes. You could glue and screw the boxes together, but you can use biscuits to avoid exposed screw heads (Photo 3). For more on using a biscuit joiner, go to familyhandyman.com and search for "biscuit." Clamp each box together (Photo 4) with a clamp at each corner and check the box with a framing square. It should automatically square itself if you've made accurate square cuts. Let the glue set for an hour before removing the clamps.

Finish and install

Finishing the boxes could be frustrating: Birch tends to get blotchy when stained, and brushing on a clear finish inside boxes is slow, fussy work. Sidestep both problems by applying two coats of golden oak penetrating oil finish.

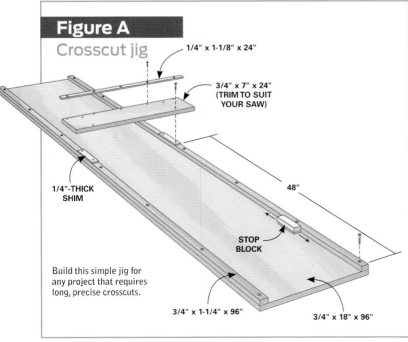

Figure A

Crosscut jig

1/4" x 1-1/8" x 24"

3/4" x 7" x 24" (TRIM TO SUIT YOUR SAW)

1/4"-THICK SHIM

48"

STOP BLOCK

Build this simple jig for any project that requires long, precise crosscuts.

3/4" x 1-1/4" x 96"

3/4" x 18" x 96"

Not just for closets!

This box system is also great for laundry rooms, garages, entryways... You can even stack the boxes to form furniture such as bookshelves or night-stands.

It leaves only a light film on the surface, so you don't have to worry about brush marks. And the light color minimizes blotching. Wipe-on poly would work well too. Use a brush to apply either finish and then wipe it with a lint-free cloth.

Once the finish is dry, join the boxes together (Photo 5). Sleeve connectors (see the Materials list) look a lot better than exposed screws. Just remember to use a Pozidriv screw tip to tighten the connectors. It may look like a Phillips, but it's slightly different. Pozidriv screw tips are available at home centers and hardware stores. You'll also need a 3/16-in. or 5mm drill bit.

To simplify mounting the boxes to the closet wall, install a cleat (Photo 6) on the wall studs about 8 in. from the floor. The 8-in. elevation keeps the boxes off the floor and provides usable space below. Make the support from long plywood scraps. The elevated ledge will support the assemblies while you get them placed and then screwed to the wall studs. Drive 2-1/2-in. screws through the box backs and the studs. If a box doesn't land on studs, use screw-in drywall anchors.

Once you have all the boxes secured to the wall, you can add closet rods (centered about 11-1/2 in. from the back wall) and other organizers like tie racks and belt hangers and screw them directly into the 3/4-in. plywood construction.

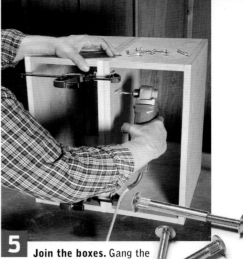

4 **Assemble boxes.** A cheap disposable paintbrush makes a good spreader. Keep a damp rag handy to wipe off excess glue.

5 **Join the boxes.** Gang the boxes together with screws or special sleeve connectors at the front and back. **SLEEVE CONNECTORS**

6 **Support the units with a cleat.** A level cleat screwed to studs makes aligning and installing the box units a lot easier. Assemble the cleat from leftover plywood scraps.

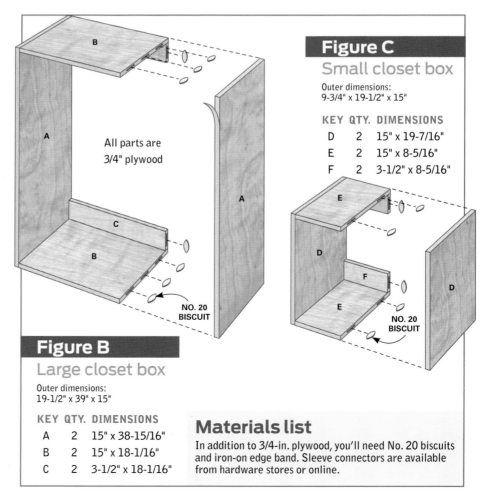

All parts are 3/4" plywood

NO. 20 BISCUIT

Figure C
Small closet box

Outer dimensions:
9-3/4" x 19-1/2" x 15"

KEY	QTY.	DIMENSIONS
D	2	15" x 19-7/16"
E	2	15" x 8-5/16"
F	2	3-1/2" x 8-5/16"

NO. 20 BISCUIT

Figure B
Large closet box

Outer dimensions:
19-1/2" x 39" x 15"

KEY	QTY.	DIMENSIONS
A	2	15" x 38-15/16"
B	2	15" x 18-1/16"
C	2	3-1/2" x 18-1/16"

Materials list

In addition to 3/4-in. plywood, you'll need No. 20 biscuits and iron-on edge band. Sleeve connectors are available from hardware stores or online.

Tie, scarf and belt organizer

Clean up a messy closet by hanging your ties, belts and scarves on this 3-in-1 closet organizer! All you need is a 2 x 2-ft. piece of 1/2-in. plywood ($10 to $15), a wooden hanger, a hook (the one shown came from the wooden hanger) and a few hours.

This organizer is 12 in. wide and 16 in. tall, but yours can be taller or narrower. To get a nice curve at the top, use the wooden hanger as a guide. Center it, trace the edge and cut it out with a jigsaw. Make a pattern of holes, slots and notches on a piece of paper and transfer it to your board. Use a 2-in. hole saw to cut the holes, making sure the board is clamped down tightly to keep the veneer from chipping (Photo 1). Use a jigsaw to cut out the side notches. To cut the slots, punch out the ends with a 5/8-in. Forstner drill bit (or a sharp spade bit) to prevent chipping, and then use a jigsaw to finish cutting out the center of each slot (Photo 2).

Sand the hanger and apply several coats of sealer or poly to smooth the edges so your scarves and ties don't snag (this is the most time-consuming step). Using a 1/4-in. round-over bit with a router makes the sanding go faster. Drill a small hole into the top of the hanger for your hook, squeeze in a bit of epoxy glue to hold it and then screw it in.

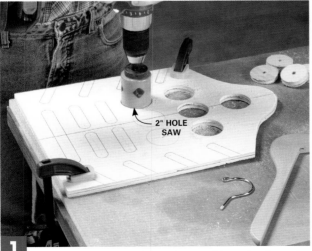

1 Drill scarf holes with a 2-in. hole saw. Clamp the plywood tightly against a piece of scrap wood to prevent chipping as the hole saw exits the plywood.

2" HOLE SAW

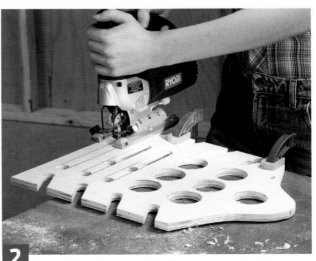

2 Use a 5/8-in. Forstner drill bit or a sharp spade bit to punch out the ends of the slots, and then finish cutting them out with a jigsaw.

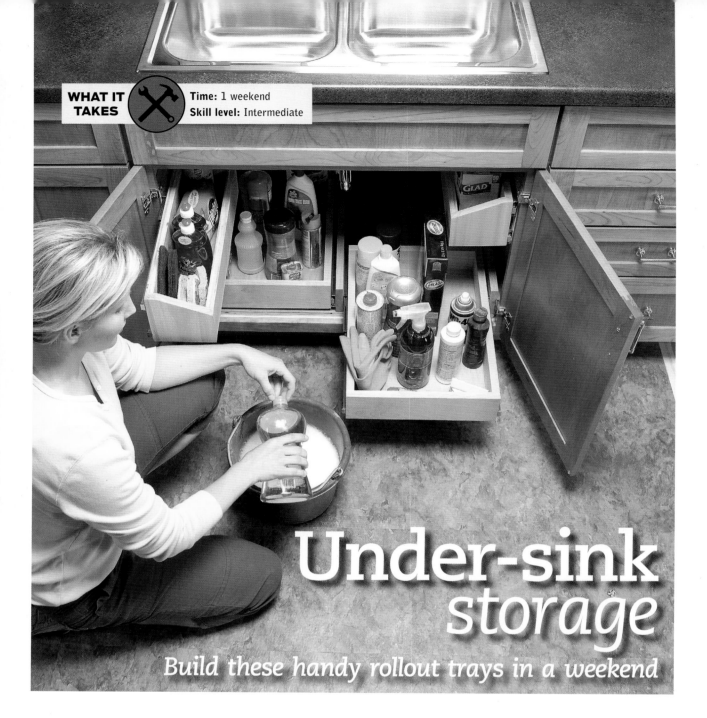

WHAT IT TAKES

Time: 1 weekend
Skill level: Intermediate

Under-sink storage

Build these handy rollout trays in a weekend

Have you finally had it with that dark and dingy, I'm-not-sure-what's-there storage space under the kitchen sink? Well, these two types of rollout trays, which ride on smooth-action ball-bearing drawer slides, will get everything out in the open and let you find exactly what you need at a glance.

This project isn't difficult. In fact, there aren't even any miter joints. All the parts are glued together and then nailed or screwed. You can make all the trays in an afternoon using building products from your local home center or hardware store for under $100.

You can build everything with simple carpentry tools and some careful measuring. You don't need a table saw for this project, but it will help you zero in on more exact measurements, especially for the lower tray bases where

accuracy is important for the ball-bearing drawer slides. The nail gun shown in the photos is also optional, but it makes assembly a lot faster and less tedious. It shoots thin 18-gauge nails.

Here, you'll learn how to measure your sink base and custom-size and assemble the wood trays. You'll also get some tips for installing the drawer slides. You'll probably have to adapt the project dimensions to fit your space. For example, you may have a bulky garbage disposer that won't allow you to install both upper slide-out trays. In that case, just make one tray instead. If you have plumbing that comes up through the floor of your sink cabinet, you may need to shorten the lower trays to fit in front of the plumbing. In any case, this project will help you organize this black hole once and for all.

Getting the right stuff

Before you get the materials, determine if you can build all the trays or only a few of them. At a home center or lumberyard, look for hardwood plywood. You can often buy 2 x 4-ft. pieces instead of a whole sheet. The hardwood plywood has two good sides and is smoother and flatter than exterior-grade softwood plywood. It costs more too.

In the hardware department, look for ball-bearing side-mount drawer slides. The pairs of the brand shown here are exactly the same—there's no specific right or left, which makes things easier if you misplace a part. Shown are 20-in.-long side-mount slides to fit 20-in.-long trays. This gives you some wiggle room in the back and a bit of extra space to get the pieces into place. If you have plumbing coming up through the bottom of the cabinet, you may need to shorten the trays and buy shorter drawer slides.

Then follow the photos for the step-by-step measuring and assembly instructions. Here are a few specifics to consider:

- If the opening between the open doors is narrower than the opening between the sides of the frame, use the shorter dimension to make the base.
- If you have a center stile or partition between the doors, you may need to make two separate bases for each side and a tray for each.
- Make sure the base and the tray parts are cut square and accurately so the trays slide smoothly.

1 Measure the width of your kitchen base cabinet inside the frame. Cut the base (A) 1/4 in. narrower than the opening.

2 Find the center of the base (A) and mark it for the center partition. Cut the 20-in.-long partitions (B) from 1x4.

Materials list

ITEM	QTY.
3/4" x 4' x 8' hardwood plywood	1
1x4 x16' maple	1
1/2" x 2' x 2' hardwood plywood	1
1x6 x 2' maple	1
20" ball-bearing drawer slides	4 prs.
Wood glue	1 pt.
Construction adhesive	1 pt.
6d finish nails, small box	1
1-5/8" wood screws, small box	1

Cutting list

(This list applies to the rollout trays shown; dimensions may vary.)

KEY	QTY.	SIZE & DESCRIPTION
A	1	3/4" x 32-3/4" x 20" plywood base
B	3	3/4" x 3-1/2" x 20" base partitions
C	2	3/4" x 12-3/4" x 18-1/2" plywood tray bottom
D	4	3/4" x 3-1/2" x 18-1/2" tray sides
E	4	3/4" x 3-1/2" x 14-1/4" tray fronts and backs
F	2	1/2" x 5-1/2" x 18-1/2" upper tray bottoms
G	2	3/4" x 5" x 18-1/2" upper tray (high side)
H	2	3/4" x 3" x 18-1/2" upper tray (low side)
J	4	3/4" x 5-1/2" x 5-1/2" upper tray front and back
K	4	1/2" x 5-1/2" x 20" side cleats (double layer)

Figure A
Sink cabinet tray detail

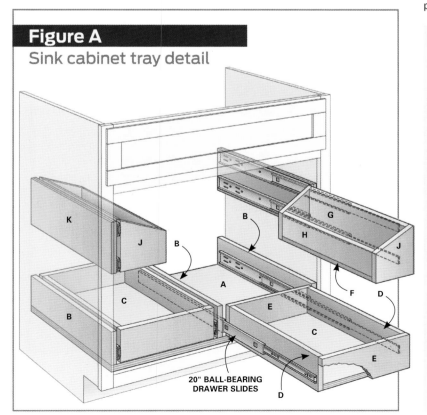

20" BALL-BEARING DRAWER SLIDES

A word about drawer slides

The ball-bearing slides are designed to mount on the sides of the trays (Photos 6 and 7). The slides require exactly 1/2 in. of space between the partition and drawer on each side to work properly, so make the trays exactly 1 in. narrower than the distance between the partitions. If the trays are too wide, they'll bind and be tough to open, in which case, you'll have to take them apart and recut the tray bottom. If the trays are too narrow, the slides will not engage. Fixing this is a bit easier. You can just shim behind the slides with thin washers.

Watch for protruding hinges and other obstructions when you mount the lower or upper trays. You may need to adjust the height or placement of the trays to accommodate them.

Seal the trays with polyurethane

You never know what kind of spill or leak will happen under the sink, so it's best to seal the wood. Once you've finished the project, remove the trays and slides, sand them with 150-grit sandpaper and brush on two coats of polyurethane. Let the trays dry thoroughly, then look through all that stuff you had stored under the sink. Toss out old stuff and combine duplicate products—and enjoy your reclaimed and now easily accessible space.

BALL-BEARING DRAWER SLIDE

RELEASE LEVER

3 Clamp the partitions to the base, drill pilot holes, and glue and screw them to the base with No. 8 x 2-in. screws.

PARTITIONS

BASE

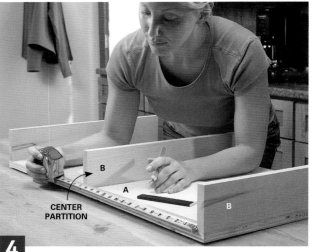

4 Measure the exact distance between the partitions. Make the outer dimension of the tray 1 in. narrower than this measurement to allow for the slides.

CENTER PARTITION

B
A
B

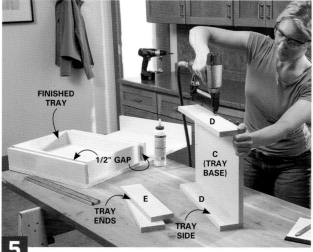

5 Cut the parts for the trays and glue and nail them together. Cut the bases perfectly square to keep the trays square.

FINISHED TRAY

1/2" GAP

D

C (TRAY BASE)

E

D

TRAY ENDS

TRAY SIDE

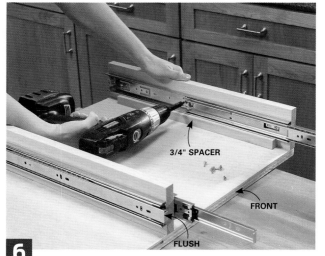

6 Set the drawer slides on 3/4-in. spacers, holding them flush with the front. Open them to expose the mounting holes and screw them to the partitions.

3/4" SPACER

FRONT

FLUSH

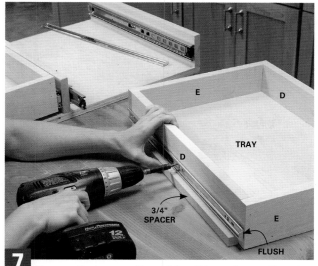

7 Remove the inner sections of the slides and screw them to the sides of the trays. Reassemble the slides and make sure they glide smoothly.

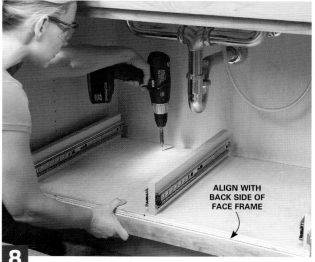

8 Insert the base assembly into the floor of the cabinet. Align the front of the base flush with the back side of the face frame. Screw the base to the floor of the cabinet.

9 Cut the parts for the upper trays, drill pilot holes, and glue and screw them together. Cut two thicknesses of plywood and glue them together to make the 1-in.-thick side cleats (K).

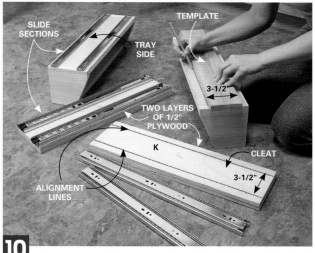

10 Cut a 3-1/2-in.-wide template, center it on the cleats and the tall side of each tray and trace the edges. Center the mounting holes of the slides on these lines and screw them to the cleats (outer sections) and tray sides (inner sections).

11 Sand the side of the cabinet to increase the adhesion, then glue and screw the cleats to the sides of the cabinet. Cut a plywood spacer to hold the cleat even.

12 Slide the upper trays into position and test the fit. Seal the trays with two coats of polyurethane to make cleaning easier.

Pegboard *and bin*

1 Cut and fasten the 2x2 frame with 3-in. drywall screws. Then screw the pegboard to the frame using 1 1/4-in. drywall screws.

1/4" PEG-BOARD
2x2 FRAME, 4' SQUARE

Probably the most essential storage item in any garage is a pegboard system. It puts your most commonly used tools within quick and easy reach. Add a bin to the bottom of the pegboard to catch all those odds and ends that don't have a home, and you won't have any excuse for not keeping your workbench or gardening bench clear of clutter.

The construction only takes about two hours. Start by cutting all the parts to size with a circular saw. See Fig. A (below) for sizes. Caution: Cut the short end caps from the long 1x6s. Don't try cutting short pieces from short boards.

Build a frame of 2x2s with one running across the center, connecting all joints with a 3-in. drywall screw. Then fasten 1/4-in. pegboard to the frame (Photo 1). One-quarter inch has a little more heft than 1/8-in. and the larger hooks it requires stay put better. Some home centers and lumber yards stock the pegboard prefinished in white. If you can find it, it's worth it. It'll brighten up the garage and save you painting time.

The trickiest part is attaching the front edge to the shelf. Using a couple of small bar clamps takes the frustration out of this step (Photo 2). Align the 1x4 front edge so it's 1/2 in. down from the shelf and clamp it to the pegboard and frame. Set back the shelf with that same 1/2-in. reveal. This 1/2-in. reveal strengthens the shelf. Predrill your screw holes with a 1/8-in. bit.

Next attach the end caps (Photo 3) to secure the shelf to the frame and to keep the front edge from tipping forward.

Finally, mount the pegboard low enough so you can easily reach your tools (Photo 4). If you're working alone, level and screw a 2x6 to the studs to temporarily support the pegboard while you attach it to the wall. Drive 3-in. screws through each member of the frame into every stud the pegboard covers.

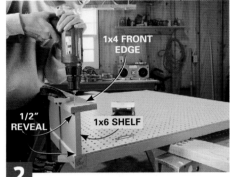

1x4 FRONT EDGE
1/2" REVEAL
1x6 SHELF

2 Clamp the 1x4 front edge and 1x6 shelf board to the frame using two small bar clamps. Screw the front ledge to the shelf with 2-in. drywall screws spaced 12 in. apart.

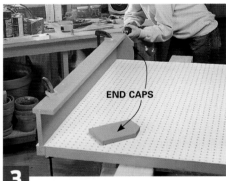

END CAPS

3 Attach end caps to each shelf with six 2-in. screws, two driven into each component.

2x6 TEMPORARY SUPPORT

4 Fasten the pegboard to the wall with 3-in. drywall screws driven through the frame into the wall studs.

WHAT IT TAKES

Time: 2 hours
Skill level: Beginner

Figure A
PEGBOARD AND SHELF DETAILS

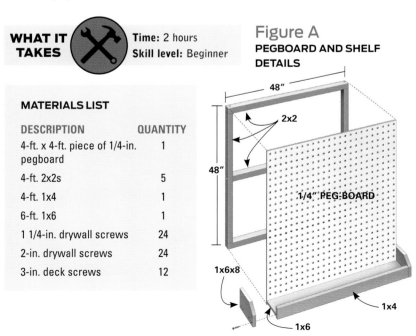

48"
48"
2x2
1/4" PEG-BOARD
1x6x8
1x4
1x6

MATERIALS LIST

DESCRIPTION	QUANTITY
4-ft. x 4-ft. piece of 1/4-in. pegboard	1
4-ft. 2x2s	5
4-ft. 1x4	1
6-ft. 1x6	1
1 1/4-in. drywall screws	24
2-in. drywall screws	24
3-in. deck screws	12

Circular saw jigs
for table saw–quality cuts

If you have a full-size table saw, you're all set for making plywood cuts. And if you have a portable table saw, you can use it for smaller ripping jobs like making shelving and drawer parts. But you can also do a fine job with only a circular saw fitted with a cabinet-grade, smooth-cutting blade and a couple of simple, screw-together jigs made from cheap melamine closet shelving stock.

WHAT IT TAKES **Time:** 1 hour
Skill level: Beginner

Ripping jig

Use an 8-ft. length of 16-in.-wide shelving to build the ripping jig. Draw a line 3 in. from the edge and cut along it with the circular saw. Screw this piece to the larger piece about 3 in. away from one edge with the factory edge facing the widest section of shelving as shown. Then use that edge as a guide to cut off the melamine. Now it's just a matter of lining up that edge with marks on plywood stock and clamping it to make perfect cuts up to 8 ft. long on any piece of plywood.

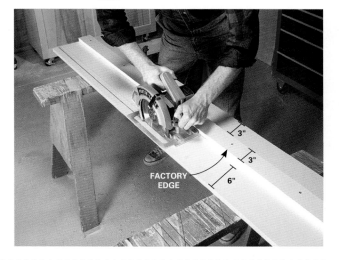

3"
3"
6"
FACTORY EDGE

STOP
4"
FACTORY EDGE

FENCE
6"
FACTORY EDGE

Crosscutting jig

You can use the ripping jig for crosscutting, too, but this crosscutting jig has the advantage of a stop on the bottom. Push the stop against the plywood, align it with the cutting mark and clamp for quick, accurate crosscuts. Make it from a 4-ft. length of 24-in.-wide melamine shelving (or plywood if wide shelving isn't available). Cut a 4-in.-wide strip for the stop from one end and another 4-in.-wide strip from one edge for the fence. Align the factory edge of the short piece with the factory edge at the other end of the shelving to make the stop. Then clamp and screw the two pieces together while checking alignment with a carpenter's square. Flip the jig over and measure from the long factory edge 6 in. to position and screw the long saw guide as shown. The key with both jigs is to use the straight factory edges for guiding the saw.

Super simple bookcase

Time: 1 weekend
Skill level: Beginner

Build it yourself and save $151,900!

This bookcase is inspired by a Gustav Stickley model that sold for $12 in 1910. One of the original Stickley models recently sold for $152,000, but you can build ours for about $100.

We built this craftsman-style bookcase with nothing more than a table saw, a drill and a pocket hole jig. If you don't own a pocket hole jig, you owe it to yourself to buy one. Pocket screws aren't as strong as most other types of joinery, but they are plenty strong for this bookcase, and you can't beat their speed and simplicity; plus you can buy a complete pocket hole system for $40. For tips on using pocket screws, go to familyhandyman.com and search for "pocket screws." You'll also need at least four pipe clamps for this project.

Wood selection matters

At the home center, we took our time picking through the oak boards. We wanted straight, flat boards, of course, but we also looked closely at grain pattern. Novice woodworkers usually skip this tedious process, but they shouldn't. It has a big impact on the final look of the project. For the legs, we examined the end grain and chose boards with grain that ran diagonally across the ends (see Photo 4). This "rift sawn" wood has straight grain on both the face and the edge of the board. ("Plain sawn" boards typically have wilder grain on the face.) Straight grain will give the legs a look that suits the Stickley style. Also, glue joints disappear in straight grain wood, so the legs—which are made from sandwiched boards—look better. For that same reason, we chose boards with straight grain along the edges to form the bookcase top (see Photo 11).

Build a box and add face frames

After cutting the plywood box parts to size (see the Cutting List), we added the 3/8-in.-thick edging (J) to protect the bottom of the cabinet sides (A; Photo 1). We applied the same edging (H) to the plywood shelves (C). Then we drilled the pocket holes in the box top and bottom (B; Photo 2). After that, we drilled holes

This is the perfect first-time furniture project—simple, useful and satisfying.

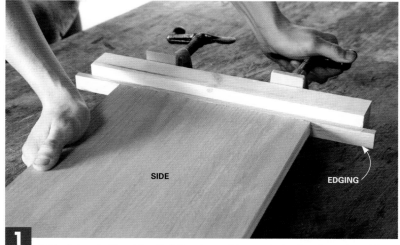

1 **Add edging to the sides.** Cut the plywood box parts to size, then glue strips of wood to the bottom edges of the box sides. This edging keeps the plywood veneer from chipping. Trim off the excess edging with a handsaw and sand it flush with the plywood. Take care not to sand through the thin veneer.

SIDE   EDGING

2 **Drill pocket holes.** Pocket hole jigs are super easy to use: Place the jig where you want the holes; clamp and drill. The stepped bit bores a pocket hole and a pilot hole at the same time. The holes on the ends are for attaching the top to the sides. The holes along the front and back are used to attach the box to the face frame.

JIG   POCKET HOLES   STEPPED BIT

3 **Assemble the box.** Drive in the pocket screws with a drill. To avoid stripping the screws in plywood and softwoods, switch to a screwdriver for the final tightening. Long clamps make assembly easier, but they aren't absolutely necessary.

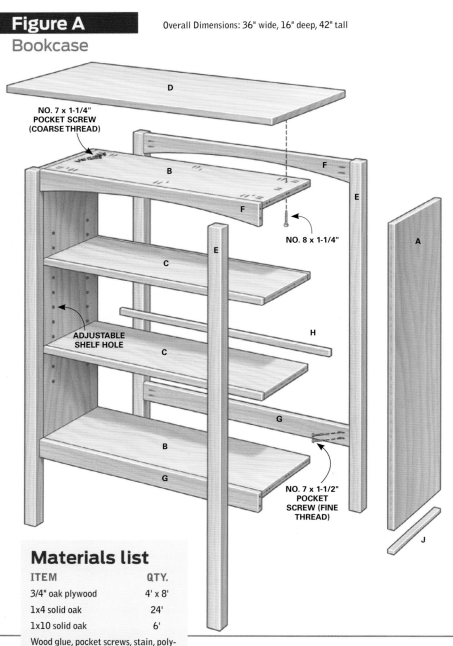

Figure A
Bookcase

Overall Dimensions: 36" wide, 16" deep, 42" tall

D

NO. 7 x 1-1/4"
POCKET SCREW
(COARSE THREAD)

F

F

E

B

F

NO. 8 x 1-1/4"

E

A

C

ADJUSTABLE
SHELF HOLE

H

E

C

G

B

G

NO. 7 x 1-1/2"
POCKET
SCREW (FINE
THREAD)

J

Materials list

ITEM	QTY.
3/4" oak plywood	4' x 8'
1x4 solid oak	24'
1x10 solid oak	6'

Wood glue, pocket screws, stain, polyurethane, adjustable shelf supports

Cutting list

MATERIAL	KEY	QTY.	DIMENSION	NOTES
3/4" Oak Plywood	A	2	10-1/2" x 32"	Sides
	B	2	10-1/2" x 29-3/4"	Top and bottom
	C	2	9-1/2" x 29-5/8"	Adjustable shelves
3/4" Oak	D	1	16" x 36"	Top
	E	4	1-1/2" x 1-1/2" x 41-1/4"	Legs (double up 3/4" stock)
	F	2	2-1/2" x 29"	Arched rails
	G	2	2" x 29"	Bottom rails
	H	4	1/2" x 29-5/8"	Edging for adjustable shelves
	J	2	3/8" x 10-1/2"	Bottom edge sides

for adjustable shelf supports in the plywood sides and—finally—we assembled the box (Photo 3).

With the box assembled, we turned our attention to building two identical face frames. (Since the bookcase has no back, it needed two face frames.) Unlike a standard face frame, which has vertical stiles, our face frame has legs (E) made from two layers of 3/4-in.-thick boards. We glued up the leg blanks (Photo 4), ripped both blanks into two legs and sanded out the saw marks.

Many beginning woodworkers figure that curves are complicated, and are a little intimidated by the arched upper rails (F). But there's a neat trick for marking out a shallow arch (Photo 5). Your curved cut (Photo 6) may not be perfect, but a little sanding will smooth it out (Photo 7).

After the rails and legs are complete, drill pocket holes in the rails and assemble the face frames (Photo 8). It's easy to make mistakes during face frame assembly, so—before driving any screws—we clamped the frames together, then set them on the box to make sure everything was aligned correctly. We used similar caution when we finally attached the face frames to the box: We dry-fitted the face frames (Photo 9) before we glued and clamped them into place (Photo 10).

Top it off and finish up

The top (D) is made by edge-gluing two boards together (Photo 11), but there are a few tricks that make it easier. First, always do a complete dry run by clamping up the boards without glue. That will alert you to any clamping or alignment problems before it's too late. Second, start with boards that are an inch or so longer than the final top.

4 **Glue up the leg blanks.** Sandwich two 1x4s together and later cut the legs from this stock. Use scrap wood "cauls" to distribute clamping pressure evenly.

CAUL

LEG BLANK

5 **Mark the arches.** Make an "arch bow"—simply a 3/16-in.-thick strip of wood with slots cut into both ends. Hook a knotted string in one slot, tighten the string to bend the bow and tie off the other end.

ARCHED RAIL

6 **Cut the arches.** For a smooth cut, use a fine-tooth blade and move slowly, putting only light forward pressure on the saw. If your saw is variable speed, cut at full speed. If the saw has orbital action, switch it off.

7 **Sand the arches.** Smooth the arches with an orbital sander. Keep the sander moving so you don't sand too deep in one spot and create a wave in the curve.

8 **Assemble the face frame.** Clamp the face frame together and drive in pocket screws. Pocket screws rarely strip out in hardwood, so you can skip the screwdriver and use only a drill.

9 **Dry-fit the face frames.** Align the face frames, pocket-screw them to the box and check the fit. If your alignment is a bit off, you can drill new pocket holes and reattach the frames. If the fit is right, you're ready to remove the face frames and add glue.

FACE FRAME

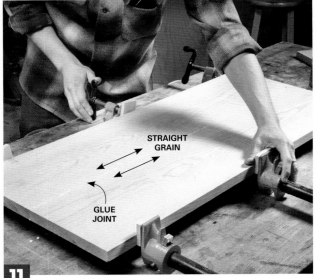

10 Glue on the face frames. Apply a light bead of glue over the box edges and screw on the face frames as before. There are no screws fastening the legs to the box sides, so you'll need to clamp them.

STRAIGHT GRAIN

GLUE JOINT

11 Glue up the top. Edge-glue the boards together to form the top. Choose boards that have straight grain lines along one edge and place those edges together. A glue joint with straight grain on both sides is almost invisible.

12 Drill slotted screw holes. Drill screw holes in the shelf box to fasten the bookcase top. Rock the bit back and forth to bore enlongated slots that will allow the top to swell with changes in humidity.

It's much easier to trim the boards later than to fuss with edge alignment during glue-up. Finally, to ensure that the tops of the boards meet flat and flush, use pocket screws on the underside of the top. A couple of pocket screws won't provide enough pressure to substitute for clamps, but they will hold the board flush while you crank on the clamps.

When the top is trimmed to size and sanded, drill elongated holes (Photo 12) and screw on the top (Photo 13). Then remove the top. Finishing is always easier when furniture is disassembled, and more important, both sides of the top need to be finished. Wood absorbs and releases moisture as humidity changes. Wood finishes slow that process. So wood with a finish on only one side will end up with differing moisture levels in the finished and unfinished sides. That leads to warping.

Finish both sides of the top (and the rest of the bookcase) with a coat of stain followed by polyurethane. That's it. Not bad for a weekend of woodworking.

13 Screw on the top from below. Drive the screws snug, but not so tight that they won't allow for seasonal wood movement. Remove the top for sanding and finishing.

Rustic shelf

Bring a bit of nature indoors with this simple branch-supported shelf. You'll have to find two forked branches about 1 in. in diameter, with one relatively straight side that will sit as flush to the wall as possible. We trimmed our branches from a crab apple, but you can use any smooth-barked tree. Our shelf is 12-in. melamine closet shelving with the ends painted white. Yours can be any wood you like, but keep the width to 12 in. or less.

To make square cuts on the branch ends, create a jig with scrap wood and a 2x4. Clamp the jig to your workbench. Then clamp each branch to the 2x4 and use the bottom edge of the jig to guide your cuts (Photo 1). Cut the branches above the crotch where the ends will be wide enough to support the shelf—one near the wall, the other close to the edge.

Clamp the shelf to the jig and trace around the branch. Drill pilot holes near the bottom of the marks at the front edge of the shelf so the screw tips won't poke through the branch (Photo 2). Bore countersink holes for the screw heads at the top of the shelf. Then hold the branches tight to the shelf while screwing them in. Hold the shelf level while you drill two holes through each branch into the drywall to mark the wall for drywall anchors. Screw your new shelf to the wall and fill it with your treasures.

WHAT IT TAKES

Time: 2 hours
Skill level: Beginner

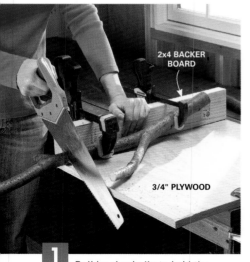

2x4 BACKER BOARD

3/4" PLYWOOD

1 Build a simple jig to hold the branch steady. Cut the ends flush with the end of the jig.

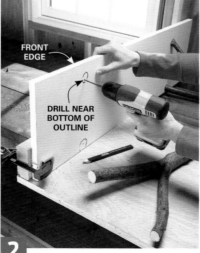

FRONT EDGE

DRILL NEAR BOTTOM OF OUTLINE

2 Trace around the branches where they touch the shelf bottom, then drill the holes and screw the shelf to the branches.

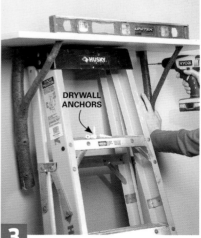

DRYWALL ANCHORS

3 Drill pilot holes near the top and bottom of the branch into the drywall. Then sink drywall anchors and screw the shelf to the wall.

Storage cabinet

This handsome cabinet is actually made from two inexpensive, unfinished cabinets purchased from a home center. The two cabinets are joined together with oak plywood and strips of solid oak, turning them into a new, larger cabinet. Use it to store books, small appliances, games and more. Assembly is amazingly fast and easy when you use a brad nailer and glue. Materials cost about $175.

First, screw the face frames of the two cabinets together. Drill pilot holes and drive screws through the lower face frame into the upper. Then lay them on one side and hold a straightedge across the fronts of the face frames to be sure they form a straight, flat surface. Slip a strip of cardboard between the two cabinet boxes to get the face frames aligned.

Next, add spacer strips that match the thickness of the protruding edge of the face frames. Cut strips just a hair thicker than 1/4 in. from a 2x4. Cutting thin strips on a table saw can be tricky, even dangerous. For tips, go to familyhandyman.com and search for "ripping safely."

Fasten the strips with plenty of glue and a few brad nails. Then add the side panel (Photo 1). Make sure the front edge of the panel is perfectly flush with the face frames, and remember that the panel overhangs the lower cabinet by 1 in. Follow the same steps on the other side.

Lay the unit on its back and check that the doors are centered on the cabinets and in line with each other

1 **Cover the sides.** Screw two cabinets together and glue spacer strips to the sides. Then glue on the side panels. Tack the panel into place, positioning nails where they'll be hidden by the legs or rails later.

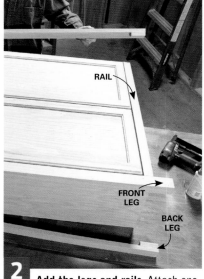

2 **Add the legs and rails.** Attach one of the front legs, then dry-fit the rails and the other leg. When they all fit right, glue and tack them in place. Follow the same dry-fit routine for the side rails and the back legs.

3 **Top it off.** Glue the two layers of the top together. To attach the top, drive screws from inside the cabinet, through the fillers and into the top.

before you add the legs and rails. The doors on these cabinets were a mess—we had to slip paper spacers behind one of the hinges and completely reinstall another.

Now you're ready to glue and nail on the legs and rails (Photo 2). Glue front leg parts (L, M and N) together, then add them to the cabinet. The top rail (T) is too thin to nail to the face frame, so just nail it to the center stile (S) and clamp it in place until the glue sets. Then remove the doors, finish-sand the whole chest and add the top, which is just two layers of plywood edge-banded and glued together (Photo 3).

Materials list

ITEM	QTY.
12" x 15" x 30" cabinet	1
12" x 30" x 30" cabinet	1
3/4" x 4' x 8' oak plywood	1
1x6 oak	30'
Edge band, knobs, wood glue, 2" screws, Early American stain, wipe-on poly	

Cutting list

KEY	QTY.	SIZE & DESCRIPTION
A	1	12" x 30" x 15" cabinet
B	1	12" x 30" x 30" cabinet
C	1	3/4" x 13-3/4" x 35" top*
D	1	3/4" x 13-1/8" x 33-3/4" sub top*
E	2	3/4" x 3" x 28-1/4" fillers*
F	4	1-1/2" x 45" spacers (thickness varies)
G	2	3/4" x 12" x 46" side panels*
H	4	3/4" x 1-1/2" x 9-1/4" side rails
J	2	3/4" x 1-3/4" x 49" back legs
K	2	3/4" x 1-3/4" x 3" back leg blocks
L	2	3/4" x 1" x 3" front leg blocks
M	2	3/4" x 1" x 49" front leg sides
N	2	3/4" x 1-3/4" x 49" front legs
P	1	3/4" x 1-1/2" x 30" rail backer*
Q	1	3/4" x 1-1/2" x 29-1/2" bottom rail
R	1	3/4" x 5/8" x 29-1/2" middle rail
S	1	3/4" x 7/8" x 14-3/8" stile
T	1	3/4" x 1/4" x 29-1/2" top rail

*Plywood parts

Figure A
Storage cabinet

Overall dimensions: 50-1/2" tall x 35" wide x 13-3/4" deep

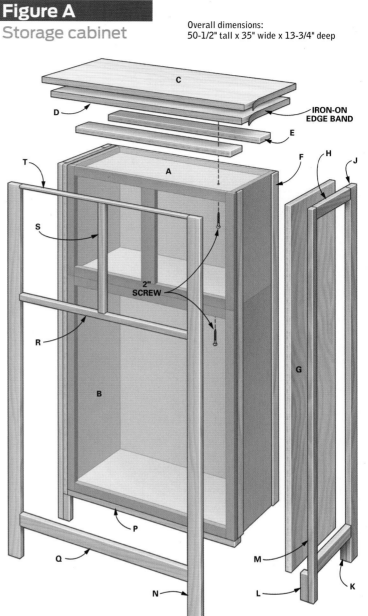

IRON-ON EDGE BAND

2" SCREW

Cheap trick: Edge banding

Every cheapskate should learn how to use iron-on edge band. It's the easiest way to cover plywood edges, and it makes inexpensive plywood look like solid wood. The top on this chest, for example, used less than $20 worth of plywood. Solid wood would have cost more than twice as much. To see how easy it is, go to familyhandyman.com and search for "edge band."

EDGE BAND

Stone waterfall

There are a thousand ways to build a backyard fountain. But if you're looking for simplicity, you can't beat this approach. You basically dig a hole in the ground, line it with rubber membrane and cover it with a stack of rocks. The waterfall looks beautiful, but the best part is the sound. If you close your eyes, it's easy to imagine yourself sitting next to a gurgling creek in the middle of the woods.

Once the materials were in hand, the project took less than a day. We were a little surprised at how much digging there was, considering the size of the reservoir. But this was the only tough part. Stacking the stone was fun. We had to rearrange the stones a few times, but in the end the water flowed nicely over the edges and created just the effect we wanted.

WHAT IT TAKES

Time: 1 day
Skill level: Beginner

Gather your supplies ahead of time

Check local landscape suppliers and home centers to find the stone, pump and pond liner. You can also order a pump online. A home center or lumberyard will have the treated lumber, rebar, hardware cloth and miscellaneous hardware you'll need. We spent about $150 for 700 lbs. of bluestone and $125 on the remaining items.

Pick out your stones

You'll need a minivan or truck to haul this much stone, or you'll have to make several trips with your car. At the stone yard, start by finding a large, flat stone for the base. Ours was about 24 in. across. Then stack stones on top in an arrangement you like. When you think you've got enough, add a few more for good measure. Don't forget to pick up three or four 5-gallon buckets full of crushed stone for the base. For this we used gray stones that ranged from 2 to 2-1/2 inches in diameter.

Dig the hole and build the frame

Using 2x8s like we did, you'll need a hole that's about 8 in. deep. In our garden, stone walls limited the size of our reservoir to about 30 in. across, but if you have room, make it bigger. The bigger the reservoir, the less often you'll have to fill it with water.

The first step is to cut the 2x8s to length and nail or screw them together. Use stainless steel or corrosion-resistant screws. Set the frame in the hole and level it (Photo 1). Then spread a 1-in. layer of sand over the bottom. Cut a square of pond liner about 2 ft. wider and longer than the inside dimensions of the frame and lay it in place. Fold the pond liner to fit the inside corners and let the extra drape down the outside of the frame. From the leftover material, cut a 20-in. square of pond liner and lay it in the center as padding for the two concrete blocks. Then set the two concrete blocks into place and wiggle them into the sand until the tops are level with the edges of the frame. The blocks will support the weight of the stones.

Next cut pieces of 1/2-in. rebar to span the reservoir. A hacksaw will work, but it's slow going. An angle grinder with a metal-cutting disc is a better option. Attach the rebar with 1/2-in. copper plumbing straps (Photo 2). When you're done, cover the rebar with galvanized 1/4-in. hardware cloth. Bend the hardware cloth down around the outside edges of the box to hold it in place and hide sharp edges.

Cut an access hole in the hardware cloth about 8 in. square and between two lengths of rebar. Once again, fold the edges of the hardware cloth down to hide sharp edges. Use this hole to install the pump. Cut another piece of hardware cloth to set over the hole so you can cover it with gravel. You'll use this access hole to clean out the reservoir occasionally and to remove the pump in the winter if you live in a cold climate.

1 **Dig a hole and lay in a wooden frame.** Add or remove dirt from under the frame to level it. Remove rocks, dirt chunks and other debris from the dirt and rake it roughly level. Pour a 1/2- to 1-in. layer of sand over the dirt and level it out.

2 **Line the frame and add rebar.** Lay the pond liner in the frame and fold the corners. Set the two concrete blocks in the center. Attach lengths of rebar about every 8 in. Complete the reservoir by adding a layer of hardware cloth.

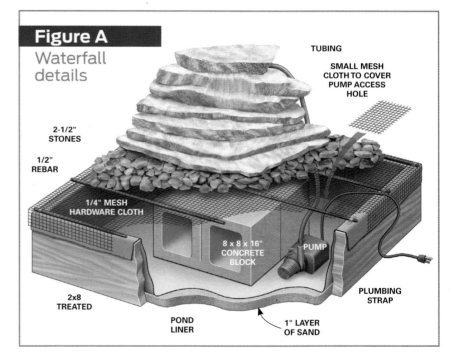

Figure A
Waterfall details

TUBING

SMALL MESH CLOTH TO COVER PUMP ACCESS HOLE

2-1/2" STONES

1/2" REBAR

1/4" MESH HARDWARE CLOTH

8 x 8 x 16" CONCRETE BLOCK

PUMP

PLUMBING STRAP

2x8 TREATED

POND LINER

1" LAYER OF SAND

Materials list

- 600 to 700 lbs. of flat stone
- Three 5-gallon buckets of crushed stone
- Two 60-lb. bags of sand
- Five 3- or 4-ft. lengths of 1/2-in. rebar
- Two 8 x 8 x 16-in. concrete blocks
- Pond liner (depending on the size of your reservoir)
- Ten 1/2-in. copper plumbing straps
- 12 corrosion-resistant 3-in. screws

- 20 corrosion-resistant 1-1/2-in. screws
- Two 2x8s, 8 ft. or longer (depending on the size of your reservoir)
- Water feature pump (see "Buying the pump," p. 84)
- Three or 4 ft. of plastic tubing—match the tubing size to the outlet on your pump
- One small stainless steel band clamp
- One or two blocks of duct seal putty—you'll usually find this in the electrical department.

3 **Build the waterfall.** Spread a layer of gravel over the hardware cloth. Then start stacking the stone. Pour water over the stones occasionally to see how it's flowing.

Stack the stone

Now for the fun part—building the waterfall. Spread the stone out near the reservoir so you can choose the size and shape you want. Start the stack with your large base stone. Stack a few stones, then pour some water over them to see how it flows (Photo 3). You can adjust the position of the stone, or choose a different one, until you get a flow pattern you like.

Install the pump and watch the water flow

Connect the pump to a length of tubing with a hose clamp. Allow enough tubing to reach from the bottom of the reservoir to the top center of the stone stack. Set the pump in the reservoir and route the tubing to the top in the least conspicuous place. Photo C at right shows how we held the tubing in place and directed the water to the front of the waterfall with duct seal putty. The duct seal putty also prevents the tubing from being crushed by the top stone.

Buying the pump

We made the mistake of starting off with a pump that was too small and were unhappy with the amount of water flowing. We recommend a pump with a flow rate of at least 300 gallons per hour and a "lift" or "head" of at least 6 ft.

If you don't have a GFCI outlet within reach of the pump cord, consider buying a low-voltage pump instead. It'll cost a little more because in addition to the pump you have to purchase a transformer (about $35), but that's a small price to pay to avoid digging a deep trench.

Buy low-voltage pumps online, or ask at the local landscape supplier. You can mount the transformer near the outlet and run low-voltage wire to the pump. Low-voltage wire only needs to be buried a few inches. Running new wiring for a 120-volt pump requires an electrical permit and a much deeper trench.

Now for the moment of truth. Fill the reservoir with water and plug in the pump. It may take a few seconds at first for the pump to start moving the water. When it does, see how it flows and make final adjustments by shimming the stones (Photo B at right).

Keep an eye on the waterfall for the first day or two to get a feel for how often you have to refill the reservoir. On hot, windy days, it may run low quickly. In cold climates, remember to bring the pump inside in the winter so it isn't damaged by freezing.

Fine-tuning techniques

If the water isn't flowing the way you'd like, here are a few tips to try. You can cause the water to drip rather than follow the underside of the stone by cutting a drip groove (Photo A). If the water isn't running in the right direction, shim under the stone to tilt it and redirect the water flow (Photo B). You can also create a dam with duct seal putty (Photo C) to block or change the water flow.

A **Cut a drip groove for better flow.** Create a better waterfall effect by cutting a groove on the underside of flat stones. The groove causes the water to drip rather than flow back along the underside of the stone.

B **Shim with small stones.** Redirect the water by tilting the stones with small shims. Just lift the stone and wedge the shim underneath.

C **Reroute water with a dam.** Make a dam out of duct seal putty to prevent water from rolling off the back of the waterfall. Here we also used the putty to secure the tubing between the top two stones.

Path *in a wheel-barrow*

There's no heavy lifting, no fancy tools and it's really, really cheap!

This garden path is as easy to build as it is to look at and walk on. A bundle or two of cedar shakes, a roll of landscape fabric, a few bags of mulch and a couple of hours are all it takes to build it.

To create the path edging, we cut 18-in.-long cedar shakes in half, then pounded the 9-inch sections about halfway into the ground. Shakes are naturally rot-resistant and should last 5 to 10 years or more. And since they're tapered, they're easy to install. Bear in mind, shakes will split and break if you try to pound them into soil with lots of rocks, roots or heavy clay; this path works best in loose garden soil.

The landscape fabric helps prevent weeds from growing up into the path and creates a barrier so the dirt below remains separate from the path materials above. The path material itself can be wood chips, shredded bark, decorative stone—just about anything you can think of.

Here's how to do it in three easy steps:

TIP:
Place a scrap 2x6 on top of each shake and pound on that if you find you're breaking shakes as you drive them in. The 2x6 will help distribute the blow more evenly across the top of the shake.

WHAT IT TAKES
Time: 2 hours
Skill level: Beginner

1 Pound the cedar shakes into the soil using a small mallet. Stagger every other shake, overlapping the previous shake by about 1/2 in.

2 Trim or fold the fabric so it follows the contour of the cedar shake edging. On sloped ground, use U-shaped sod staples to hold the fabric.

3 Install a 2- to 3-in. layer of wood chips, shredded bark or stone over the landscape fabric.

Pebble mosaic steppers

Collect some river rock and make your own unique stepping-stone path

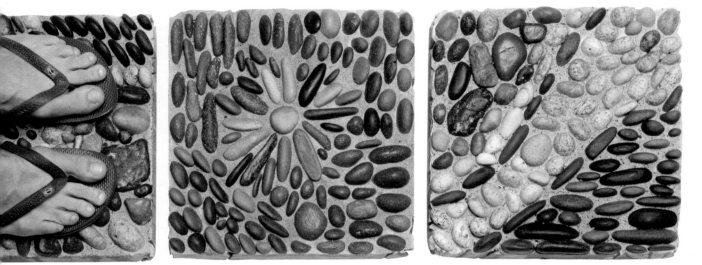

Love to collect pebbles? You can use them to make these beautiful pebble mosaic stepping-stones using a "dry-set" technique that makes it easy to change or adjust the pattern as you go without having to dig the stones out of wet mortar.

In addition to showing you how to make these stepping-stones, we've included plans for an ingenious reusable wooden mold. The initial investment for this project—about $50—gets you the plywood, a bag of mortar, pigment and muriatic acid. It's enough material to make about seven or eight stepping-stones. After that, each one will cost you less than a dollar.

Build the mold

A small sheet of 3/4-in. plywood and some 1-1/4-in. screws are all you'll need to build the mold. Cut out the pieces according to the Cutting List. Figure A shows how the parts go together. When you're done, brush linseed or vegetable oil on the mold to protect it from moisture.

Start by collecting the stones

We found these stones on the north shore of Lake Superior. You'll find similar stones in most parts of the country. Look for them in river and creek beds or along lakeshores. Wherever you find them, make sure you have permission and that it's legal to collect them. Another possible source is your local landscape supplier or wherever landscaping stone is sold.

For this project, we sorted them by color, filling buckets and cans full of red, gray, white, brown and speckled stones. Keeping them sorted makes it a lot easier to find the right one as you create a pattern.

Assemble the stepping-stone

Photos 1–4 show the assembly steps. Add a little brown pigment to the dry Type S mortar mix to give the stepping-stones a mellower look. You'll find cement pigments and Type S mortar at home centers and masonry suppliers. Or you can cheat and just mix in a little colored ceramic tile grout. Make sure to wear rubber gloves to protect your skin from the mortar, which can cause skin burns.

You don't have to plan your pattern ahead of time. Just think of a design and start arranging the stones. It's easier to start along the edges or in a corner and work toward the center, though. You'll have less fitting to do as you fill in the last few stones. Keep the stones close together and oriented with the long axis up and down. While it's tempting, avoid laying a stone flat. It doesn't look as good as you think it will and is more likely to pop out later. When you're done tamping the stones into the dry mortar, inspect the space between the stones to see if there are spots that require more mortar. They should be buried at least halfway. Fill sparse areas with more mortar. Dust any dry mortar off the stones with a small brush.

Figure A
Stepping-stone mold
(forms 12" square steppers)

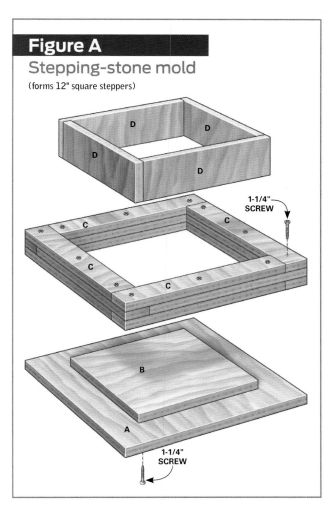

1-1/4"
SCREW

1-1/4"
SCREW

You can just pull out the rocks and wipe the slate clean if you don't like the design.

1 **Assemble the mold.** This plywood mold goes together quickly and comes apart easily after the mortar hardens. And you can use it again and again.

The trickiest part of the process is wetting the mortar (Photo 5). We can't tell you exactly how much water to add, but it's better to sprinkle on several small doses than to get impatient and risk adding too much. The key is to alternate between wetting the top and tapping on the mold with the rubber mallet until it seems like not all of the water is being absorbed and bubbles quit appearing (Photo 6). Expect to spend about 45 minutes sprinkling and tapping.

Materials list

- Collection of small stones
- One bag of Type S mortar mix
- 2' x 2' square piece of 6-mil poly
- 48" x 48" x ¾" plywood
- Forty 1-1/4" corrosion-resistant screws
- Optional items: mortar pigment or colored grout, muriatic acid and stone sealer

Cutting list

KEY	QTY.	SIZE & DESCRIPTION
A	1	18" x 18" x 3/4" subbase
B	1	12" x 12" x 3/4" base
C	12	2-1/4" x 15-3/4" x 3/4" frame
D	4	3-1/4" x 12-3/4" x 3/4" sides

WHAT IT TAKES **Time:** 4 hours
Skill level: Beginner

Some of our vast collection of rocks.

When the mortar is thoroughly dampened, set the completed stepping-stone in a shady spot and cover it with a damp cloth and plastic. Wait at least 48 hours before removing the mold.

After you remove the mold from the stepping-stone (Photo 7), brush the stone off to remove any loose mortar and rinse it with clear water. If, after drying, the embedded stones have a film of mortar on them, clean it off with muriatic acid diluted according to the instructions on the container. Remember, always add acid to water, not the other way around, and wear rubber gloves and safety glasses.

To enhance the color of the stones, coat them with stone sealer. You'll find stone sealers at home centers, masonry, landscape and tile suppliers, and online.

2 **Spread dry mortar in the form.** Fill the plastic-lined form to about 3/4 in. from the top edge with dry Type S mortar. Level it with your gloved hand. It doesn't have to be perfectly flat.

3 **Arrange stones in a pattern.** The only rule is to keep the stones close together so they touch and stand up and are not laid flat.

4 **Tamp the stones to level the tops.** Lay a board across the stones and pound on it with a rubber mallet to embed the stones in the dry mortar and set the tops level with each other.

6 **Tap on the form.** Tap on the form with the mallet to remove air and help the water penetrate. Continue sprinkling and tapping until is seems like no more water will be absorbed by the mortar.

5 **Sprinkle the stone.** Adjust your spray wand or sprayer to the finest spray setting and sprinkle water over the completed stepping-stone to wet the mortar.

7 **Pull off the mold.** Allow the stepping-stone to harden and cure for at least two days. Then carefully flip it over and remove the mold. Clean it with water and then acid if needed.

Garden rock sifter

for cleaning rock mulch

Old rock mulch gets mixed with dirt and leaves and looks terrible. To clean it up, make a garden sifter to separate the rocks from the debris. Build a 2x4 frame and fasten hardware cloth to the bottom with fence staples. Then elevate the sifter on old bricks and use a power washer to clean each shovelful of rocks. You could use a hose or shake the rocks on the sifter (but that's a lot more work!).

Island deck

Most decks are attached to houses, but there's no reason they have to be. Sometimes the best spot to set up a deck chair and relax is at the other end of the yard, tucked into a shady corner of the garden. And if you don't attach the deck to the house, you don't need deep frost footings—which can save hours of backbreaking labor, especially in wooded or rocky areas where footings are difficult to dig.

This deck was designed with simple construction in mind. If you can cut boards and drive screws, you can build it. The only power tools you'll need are a circular saw and a drill. Shown is a premium grade of low-maintenance composite decking with hidden fasteners, which brought the total cost to over $2,000, but using standard treated decking and screws would lower the cost by more than half. You may need to special-order composite decking and hidden fasteners if you use the same ones as shown here, but everything else is stocked at home centers or lumberyards.

Place the footings and beams

Lay out the two beams parallel to each other, 9 ft. apart. Screw on temporary 1x4 stretchers across the ends of the beams, overhanging them each the same distance,

Quick results

The simplicity of this deck makes it fast to build. With a helper and all the materials ready to go first thing in the morning, you can have a completed deck in 12 hours. If you add a step to your deck and use hidden deck fasteners as shown, you might need a few more hours to finish the job.

1 Lay a quick foundation with minimal digging by setting concrete blocks on gravel. Level from high to low spots with a string level.

LOW POINT

LINE LEVEL

HIGH POINT

then measure diagonally to make sure the beams are square to each other. Mark the location of the gravel base (see Figure A) by cutting the grass with a shovel, then move the beams out of the way and cut out the sod where the gravel will go.

Establish the highest and lowest points with a string and string level to get a rough idea of how deep to dig and how much gravel to put in to make the blocks level (Figure A). Tamp the dirt with a block to make a firm base, then spread the gravel. Place the blocks and level them against each other and in both directions (Photo 1), adding or scraping out gravel as needed. Use construction adhesive between the 4-in.-thick blocks if you stack them, or use 8-in. blocks. If your site slopes so much that one side will be more than 2 ft. off the ground, support it on a 4x4 post on a frost footing instead—it'll look better and be safer.

Set the beams across the blocks and square them to each other, using the same 1x4 stretchers to hold them parallel

2 Take diagonal measurements and tap one beam forward or back to square the beams. Temporary stretchers hold the beams parallel.

TEMPORARY STRETCHER

EQUAL DISTANCE

JOIST LOCATION

3 Screw on angle brackets at each joist location instead of toenailing, which can split and weaken the joists and knock the beam out of square.

and square (Photo 2). If the beams are not perfectly level, shim them with plastic or pressure-treated wood shims (sold in home centers).

Mark the joist locations on the

TIP:
If all or part of the deck is higher than 30 in. off the ground, you'll need a building permit and railings. If you intend to build any kind of structure on top of the deck or attach the deck to the house, you also need a permit. Also, keep the deck at least 4 ft. back from the property line.

Figure A
Island deck

Dimensions:
11' 8" square (not including stairs)

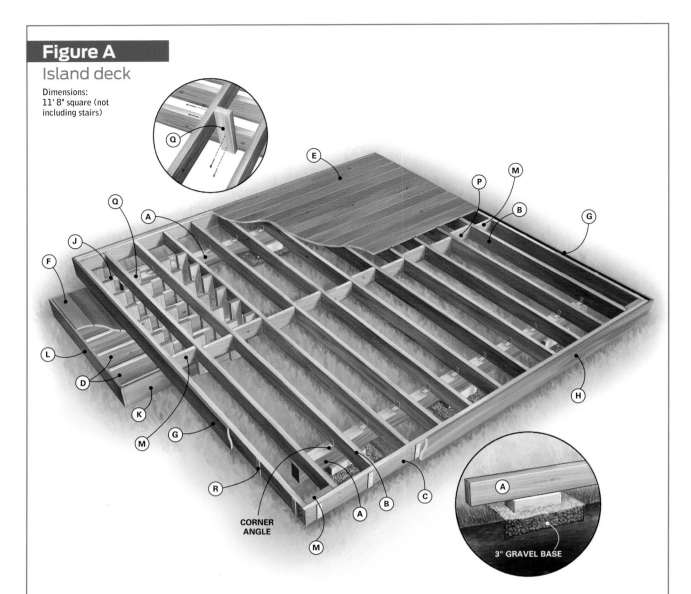

CORNER ANGLE

3" GRAVEL BASE

Materials list

ITEM	QTY.
4" x 8" x 12" solid concrete block	6 (min.)
Class 5 crushed gravel	6 bags
4x6 x 10' pressure-treated timbers	2
2x6 x 12' (12" o.c. joist spacing)	19
1-1/2" corner angles	22
7" reinforcing angles (or 2x4 x 11" blocks)	25
5/4x6 x 12' decking (Trex or other)	25
1x8 x 12' matching skirt board	5
Joist hanger nails	2 lbs.
1-5/8" deck screws	5 lbs.
3" deck screws	2 lbs.
2" stainless steel trim head screws	2 lbs.
Hidden deck fasteners (search online)	2
1x4 x 10' temporary stretchers (for layout)	2

Cutting list

KEY	QTY.	SIZE & DESCRIPTION
A	2	3-1/2" x 5-1/2" x 120" beams
B	13	1-1/2" x 5-1/2" x 135" joists
C	2	1-1/2" x 5-1/2" x 138" rim joists
D	7	1-1/2" x 5-1/2" x 48" stair stringers
E	24	1" x 5-1/2" x 138" deck boards (cut in place)
F	2	1" x 5-1/2" x 55-1/2" stair treads
G	2	3/4" x 7-1/2" x 140" skirt board
H	2	3/4" x 7-1/2" x 138-1/2" skirt board
J	1	3/4" x 7-1/2" x 48" skirt board
K	1	3/4" x 7-1/2" x 24" skirt board
L	1	3/4" x 7-1/2" x 57-1/2" riser
M	6	1-1/2" x 5-1/2" x 7-1/2" blocking
P	10	1-1/2" x 5-1/2" x 10-1/2" blocking
Q	25	1-1/2" x 3-1/2" x 11" joist supports (can be used instead of metal reinforcing angles)
R	40	1/4" x 5-1/2" spacers

 END JOIST

RIM JOIST

4 Install the middle and end joists, then screw on the rim joists, using clamps (or a helper) to hold them in place.

FASTEN FROM BOTH SIDES

5 For strong connections at the corners, set corner blocking between the last two joists, then nail the rim joist from both directions.

STRINGER

6 Frame the steps next. You can avoid additional footings by hanging stringers from the deck joists with metal angles or 2x4s.

beams, starting with a joist on the end of each beam. Shown are 11 joists spaced 12 in. on center to keep the composite decking from sagging over time, but wood decking can be spaced 16 in. on center.

Instead of toenailing, which often splits the wood, use metal angles to hold down the joists. This also makes it easy to place the joists. Attach one alongside each joist location (Photo 3).

Cantilever the joists on all sides

Set the two outer joists and the center joist on the beams against the metal angles. Extend the joists over the beam on one side by 10-1/2 in., but let them run long over the opposite beam. Trim them to exact length when

the deck is almost done so you can avoid ripping the last deck board.

Fasten the joists to the angles with deck screws. Screw on both rim joists—you'll have to take the second rim joist back off when the joists are trimmed and then reattach it, but it's needed to hold the joists straight and to hold the outside joists up (Photo 4). The decking will hold the outside joists up when the rim joist is removed later.

Set the other joists on the beams and fasten them to the beams and rim joists. Reinforce the outside corners with additional blocking (Photo 5). Finally, mark the center of the joists and run blocking between each pair of joists. Set the blocking 1/2 in. to the side of the center

7 Attach the deck boards. Decks look best when you use hidden fasteners, but they make installation slower. Trim the deck boards flush with the rim joist when you're done.

HIDDEN FASTENER

RIM JOIST

8 Wrap the deck with skirt boards that match the decking, driving trim head screws just below the surface at the spacer locations (see Figure A).

SKIRT BOARD

9 Screw skirt boards to the sides of the steps for a finished look, then measure, cut and attach a riser board to the face of the steps.

RISER

SPACER

NOTCH HERE

SKIRT BOARD

mark, alternating from side to side, so that the blocking doesn't end up in the gap between the deck boards.

Add a step

The deck surface should be no more than 8 in. above the ground where you step up on it. If it's close, just build up the ground or add concrete pavers. Otherwise, add a step.

To cantilever the stairs, extend the stair stringers underneath four deck joists, then join the floor joists and stair stringers with reinforcing angles (as shown) or wood 2x4s, which are less expensive (Photo 6). Use a screw first to hold the angles or 2x4 blocks in place, then finish fastening them with nails, which have greater shear strength.

The 5/4 (nominal) decking shown (composite decking) called for a maximum spacing between stair stringers of 9 in. on center, but you can space stringers 16 in. on center if you use solid wood.

Hidden fasteners create a clean look

The deck boards shown are attached with hidden fasteners. Various types of hidden fasteners are available—or you can use deck screws, which create lots of holes but save time and money.

Start with a full board at one side, aligning it with the edge of the rim joist. Leave the boards long at both ends, then cut them back later all at once so the edges are straight. Use four 1/4-in. spacers between each pair of boards as you fasten them, but check the distance to the rim joist after every four boards and adjust spacing if necessary.

At the next to the last board, remove the rim joist and mark and cut the ends off the joists so the last deck board lines up with the edge of the rim joist. Reinstall the rim joist and attach the last boards.

Nail 1/4-in. spacers ripped from treated wood to the rim joist every 16 in. so water won't get trapped against the rim joist. Screw on skirt boards with two screws at each spacer (Photo 8). Attach the decking to the steps after the skirt boards are fastened. Finally, finish the steps (Photo 9).

Backyard spring

Build this bubbling fountain in 4 hours

WHAT IT TAKES **Time:** 4 hours **Skill level:** Beginner

If you've ever been to Yellowstone, you probably remember the magic of the natural springs. In less than half a day, you can build your own small spring to enjoy at home. Here's what you need:

■ A large sturdy tub or bucket (about a 15-gallon size).

■ A piece of pond liner large enough to line the bucket plus an additional foot on each side. The liner shown here is 5 ft. square.

■ A small fountain pump (this one moves 210 gallons per hour).

■ A piece of flexible braided plastic tubing the diameter of the pump outlet and cut to the length of the bucket height.

■ A hose clamp to connect the tubing to the pump.

■ A brick to rest the pump on.

■ A square piece of heavy-gauge, galvanized hardware cloth with a 1/4-in. grid, cut 6 to 8 in. larger than the diameter of the bucket.

■ About 40 lbs. of round rocks 1-1/2 to 3 in. in diameter. Mexican beach pebbles from a local nursery were used here.

You can tuck this spring fountain in the corner of a patio where you can easily see and hear the water. It can go anywhere in your yard or garden, but you'll need an outdoor outlet nearby.

Dig it in

■ Dig a hole the size of your bucket, but slightly deeper. Place the top lip of the bucket 2-1/2 in. below the surface of the patio or ground.

■ Place the bucket in the hole and backfill around it.

■ Line the inside of the bucket with your pond liner. Extend the liner out at least 8 in. beyond the diameter of the bucket, more if you want your spring to shoot up higher. You want the liner to catch any water splashing on the rocks and direct the runoff back into the bucket. Curl up the edge of the liner to create a ledge for that purpose. Create a ledge by wedging the liner between two bricks.

■ Place the brick and the pump in the center of the bucket. Connect the tubing to the pump outlet with a hose clamp.

■ Follow the manufacturer's instructions for running the cord. Don't bury it. Caution: Plug the cord into a GFCI-protected outlet.

■ Place the hardware cloth over the bucket and snip a small hole in the center to allow the tubing through. The hardware cloth should be larger than the diameter of the bucket.

■ Place the stones and brick on top of the hardware cloth and fill the bucket with water.

■ Turn the pump on and adjust the tubing, wedging it between the rocks to get the desired effect. You can restrict the flow of the water by pinching the pipe with wire or buying a flow restricter from your pump supplier. The diameter of the pipe will determine how high the water bubbles up.

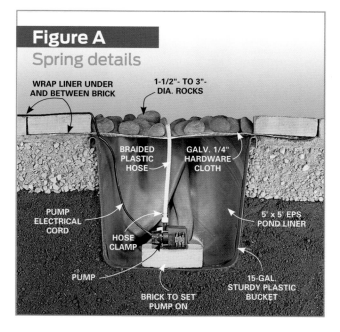

Figure A
Spring details

WRAP LINER UNDER AND BETWEEN BRICK

1-1/2"- TO 3"- DIA. ROCKS

BRAIDED PLASTIC HOSE

GALV. 1/4" HARDWARE CLOTH

PUMP ELECTRICAL CORD

HOSE CLAMP

5' x 5' EPS POND LINER

PUMP

15-GAL. STURDY PLASTIC BUCKET

BRICK TO SET PUMP ON

WHAT IT TAKES
Time: 1–2 days
Skill level: Intermediate

Add a **faucet** *anywhere in your yard*

And stop lugging that hose around

If dragging hoses around is a constant activity in your yard, install a remote faucet and eliminate that hassle forever. The job will take you a day or two (depending on how much trenching is required) and cost less than $100. Everything you'll need is available at home centers.

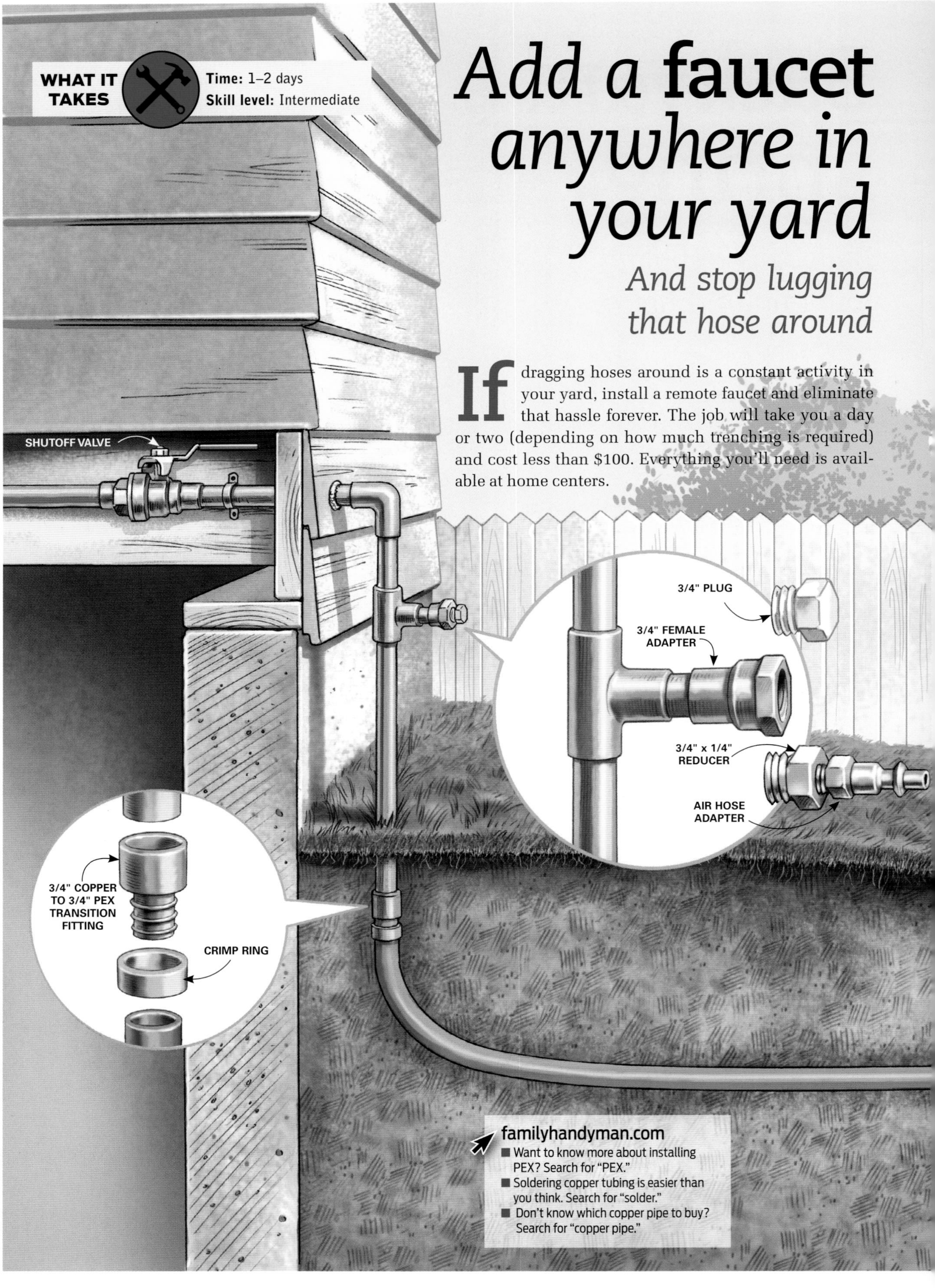
SHUTOFF VALVE
3/4" PLUG
3/4" FEMALE ADAPTER
3/4" x 1/4" REDUCER
AIR HOSE ADAPTER
3/4" COPPER TO 3/4" PEX TRANSITION FITTING
CRIMP RING

familyhandyman.com
- Want to know more about installing PEX? Search for "PEX."
- Soldering copper tubing is easier than you think. Search for "solder."
- Don't know which copper pipe to buy? Search for "copper pipe."

The inside connection

To get the best flow rate at the garden, tap into an interior 3/4-in. cold water line. If you can't find one that's convenient, tap into a 1/2-in. line instead (you'll just get a slightly lower flow rate). If you have a water softener, tap into a water line before the softener.

The trench

Call 811 a few days before you dig so the utility companies can locate buried pipes and cables in your yard. You only have to bury the water line about 6 in. deep. If you're trenching in hard clay or rocky soil, that's about as deep as you'll want to go. If you're working in soft soil, it's smart to go at least 12 in. deep to reduce the risk of future damage. At any depth, you can easily protect the water line from shovel attacks: Cover the tubing with a couple of inches of soil, then pour in about 2 in. of dry concrete mix before backfilling the trench. Soil moisture will harden the concrete.

The pipeline

Copper pipe is best for the exposed plumbing at the house, but PEX tubing is best for underground. It's a lot cheaper than copper and it's easier to install than CPVC plastic. With PEX, you can make a continuous run from your house and make turns without installing a single fitting. Plus, PEX tolerates mild freezing better than either CPVC or copper (in case you're late blowing out the line). However, you'll have to invest about $50 in a 3/4-in. PEX crimping tool. If you don't want to shell out the cash, use CPVC.

The blow-out system

If you live in a freeze zone, you'll have to blow out the system before the first hard freeze. It's easy to do with a home air compressor, but you'll have to install the components now (instead of during a snowstorm).

At the house, splice in a tee and a threaded female 3/4-in. adapter, and cap it with a plug. That's where you'll connect your compressed-air line.

At the garden, install a blow-out valve (a ball valve is best) below grade in a gravel pit. Use a sprinkler system valve box (about $15)

to cover it. Before the first freeze, close the shutoff valve and unscrew the plug. Next, screw in a standard air hose fitting and a reducer and connect your air hose. Out at the faucet, open both the faucet and the blow-out valve and let the water drain. Then, close just the faucet and blow out any remaining water with your compressor. Finally, close the blow-out valve and replug the blow-out fitting back at the house.

The post and faucet

We cut a length of hollow PVC fence post to mount the faucet, but you can build your own post out of any material. Make sure the PEX runs inside it to protect it from sunlight—UV rays reduce its life. Set the post at least 18 in. deep. Screw the sill cock flange to the post and install a screw-on backflow preventer. Note: Check with your local plumbing inspector for backflow prevention requirements in your area.

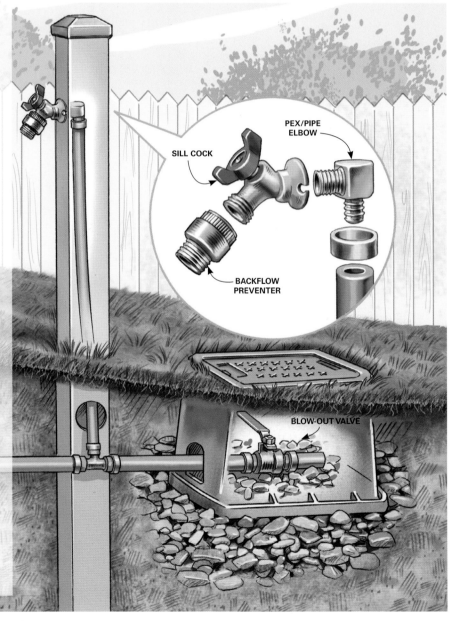

SILL COCK

PEX/PIPE ELBOW

BACKFLOW PREVENTER

BLOW-OUT VALVE

Run power anywhere in your yard

The easiest way to bring electricity to a shed, garden or lamppost

WHAT IT TAKES

Time: 1–2 days
Skill level: Advanced

Dragging extension cords across the yard to power the weed whip, fumbling around in a dark shed...most of us take these hassles for granted. But it doesn't have to be that way. With a day's work, you can run electrical lines to any part of your yard. This article will show you how to bring power to a shed, but the process is almost identical if you want to simply mount an outlet on a post planted in the soil. A licensed electrician would charge at least several hundred dollars plus materials to run lines from your house to a shed 50 ft. away (not including any work inside your house). You can do the job yourself for a materials cost of about $140.

We'll show you how to run wires through rigid metal conduit (RMC). This method offers the best protection of the wiring and requires the least amount of digging. It also lets you install a GFCI outlet at the end of the line rather than at the house, which means you'll never have to run back to the house to reset a tripped GFCI. For information on completing the wiring inside the outbuilding or connecting to power in your house, go to familyhandyman.com and search for "wiring."

If you want to provide a dedicated circuit to the shed, hire an electrician to make the final connection in your main electrical panel. Otherwise you can connect to an existing circuit if the circuit has enough capacity and the box you're connecting to has enough volume for the additional wires.

1 **Dig the trench.** Use a mattock to dig the trench. The narrow head means less dirt to remove and less to put back. Slice out strips of sod with a spade so you can neatly patch the lawn later.

SOD FOR PATCHING

8"-DEEP TRENCH

To run the wires inside rigid conduit, you'll need a hacksaw, a pipe bender capable of bending 1/2-in. rigid conduit with an outside diameter of 3/4 in., and a fish tape long enough to reach through the buried pipe. You'll also need a pair of pipe wrenches to screw the sections of pipe together, a drill and 1-in. bit capable of penetrating your siding, and wire cutting and stripping tools. The total cost of this project is typically about $2.20 for every foot of buried conduit, plus LB fittings and miscellaneous hardware.

A few weeks before you start the project, contact your local building department to obtain an electrical permit if one is required. Caution: A few days before you dig, call 811 to have your underground utility lines marked. Learn more at call811.com.

Plan the route

There are several factors to consider in planning the route from the house to the shed. Obviously the shorter the trench, the less digging you'll have to do, but you also have to determine where you're going to connect to power inside the house and how easy it will be to get there. In some cases, a little more digging could save you from having to tear into a basement ceiling. Start by locating a power source, whether it's your main panel, a ceiling box, outlet or other electrical box. Then figure out the best spot for the new conduit to enter the house. Since the National Electrical Code (NEC) limits the number of bends you can make in the pipe to a total of 360 degrees, you have to plan the route carefully. The

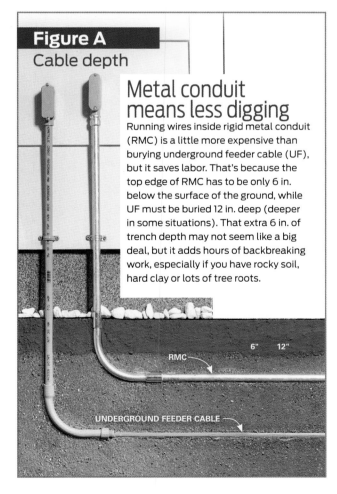

Figure A
Cable depth

Metal conduit means less digging

Running wires inside rigid metal conduit (RMC) is a little more expensive than burying underground feeder cable (UF), but it saves labor. That's because the top edge of RMC has to be only 6 in. below the surface of the ground, while UF must be buried 12 in. deep (deeper in some situations). That extra 6 in. of trench depth may not seem like a big deal, but it adds hours of backbreaking work, especially if you have rocky soil, hard clay or lots of tree roots.

RMC

6"   12"

UNDERGROUND FEEDER CABLE

2 **Plan the bend.** Measure from the bottom of the trench to the bottom of the LB fitting. Mark that measurement on the conduit.

3 **Bend the conduit.** Pull back on the conduit bender until the end stands straight up. A magnetic level lets you know when you've got a perfect 90-degree bend.

4 **Join the conduit.** Assemble the conduit run above ground to make tightening the connections easier. Support the conduit with 2x4s until you've connected all but the last section.

5 **Plan the last piece.** Measure for the last section of conduit. Adjust the measurement for the distance the LB protrudes from the wall. Then mark the pipe and bend it.

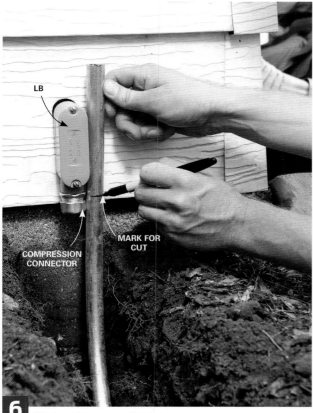

6 **Mark and connect.** Hold the bent conduit in place to mark it for cutting. Since there are no threads on the end of the pipe, screw a compression fitting into the LB and connect the conduit to it.

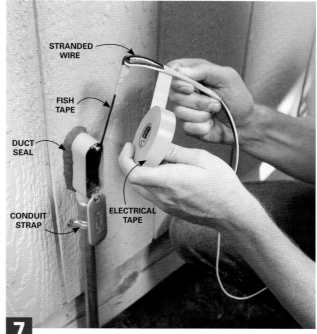

7 **Tie the wire to the fish tape.** Feed the fish tape through the conduit. Loop the wires through the fish tape and wrap them with electrical tape. Also wrap the hook on the fish tape so it can't snag. Use stranded wire, not solid wire.

two 90-degree bends from the ground into the house and shed consume 180 degrees, leaving you 180 degrees more for any additional bends.

With the route planned, you can measure for the amount of wire and conduit you need and head to the hardware store or home center. Add 10 ft. to the length of wire and pipe to make sure you'll have enough.

It's smart to drill the hole into the house before you start digging just in case you run into an obstacle and have to choose a new location. When you're sure of the exit point, dig a trench from the house to the shed. If you're going across a lawn, remove a slice of sod the width of a spade from the surface and set it aside to reuse after you bury the pipe. Then use a mattock or narrow spade to dig the trench (Photo 1). Pile the dirt on plastic tarps so you don't have to rake it out of the grass later.

Mount the LBs and metal boxes

The rigid conduit will come out of the ground and into a fitting called an "LB." The LB has a removable cover that simplifies the task of pulling wire by eliminating a sharp right-angle turn. The trickiest part of this project is mounting the LBs and connecting them to metal boxes inside the house and shed. In general, you'll have to choose a box location and then calculate the length of electrical metallic tubing (EMT) needed to reach from the back of the LB to the box. If you're going into a basement or crawl space, the length of the conduit usually

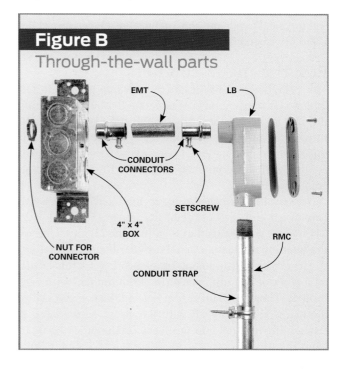

Figure B
Through-the-wall parts

isn't critical. Start by drilling a small hole with a long bit to make sure you're in the right spot. Then drill a 1-in. hole for the LB and conduit. Screw a 1/2-in. conduit connector into the back of the LB and then attach a piece of 1/2-in. EMT that's long enough to reach an easily accessible box in the basement or crawl space. After you've mounted the LB to the siding, go inside and add a conduit connector and a metal electrical box to the other end of the EMT. This box is where you'll make the connections from your house wiring to the new shed wiring.

8 **Pull the wires.** Pull the wires through the conduit. This is a two-person job—you need a helper at the other end to feed the wires into the conduit.

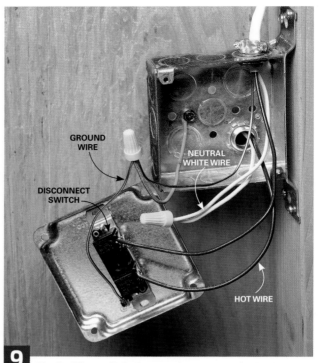

GROUND WIRE

NEUTRAL WHITE WIRE

DISCONNECT SWITCH

HOT WIRE

9 **Start with a switch.** Connect the wires inside the shed to a switch. Then run them to a GFCI receptacle.

On the inside of the shed, you'll screw a 4 x 4-in. square metal box to the side of the stud. Then connect the LB to the box using the parts shown in Figure B.

Run the metal conduit

The 10-ft. lengths of RMC are threaded on both ends and include a coupling on one end. You'll start by bending the first pipe and threading an LB onto the end. Then thread the pipes together one at a time until you reach the other end, where you'll cut and bend the last piece of conduit to fit and connect it to the LB with a compression connector. Photos 1 – 6 show the process.

Temporarily attach the LB to the shed and measure between it and the bottom of the trench (Photo 2). Add 3/4 in. for the threads that'll go into the LB and subtract the bending allowance listed on your bender (usually 6 in.) from this measurement for the bend. Mark this length on a piece of conduit, measuring from the end with bare threads. Then find a level spot to bend the conduit. Align the mark on the conduit with the arrow on the bender. Push with your foot and pull back on the pipe handle to bend the pipe (Photo 3). Use a level or the bubble built into some benders to tell when you reach 90 degrees. Take the bent conduit back to the trench and screw the LB onto the end. Photo 4 shows how to connect lengths of conduit until you reach the house.

Bend the last piece of conduit up and cut it off to fit into the compression connector (Photos 5 and 6). Start by measuring from the last piece of conduit to the house wall (Photo 5). If the LB is held away from the wall by siding, subtract this distance from the measurement. Then add 3/4 in. for the threading and subtract for the bend. Mark the last piece of conduit, starting from the

bare threads. Once again, place the bender arrow on the mark and bend the conduit. Face the threaded end of the conduit when you make this bend, not the end with the coupling. Mark the conduit (Photo 6) and cut it with a hacksaw. Remove burrs from the inside of the pipe by smoothing with a file or by inserting the bare metal handles of pliers into the pipe and twisting. Complete the conduit run by threading on the last piece of conduit. You'll have to lift the previous piece of conduit to create clearance as you spin the bent pipe around. Finally, slip the end of the conduit into the compression connector and tighten the compression nut with a wrench. Wrap a conduit strap around the conduit and screw it to the house to secure the conduit. Also press a rope of "duct seal" around the top of the LB to keep water out.

Pull the wires

Remove the covers from the LBs and push a fish tape through the conduit. Then pull the wire through the conduit (Photos 7 and 8). You'll need two wires, one white and one black, for one circuit, or more if you intend to wire a three-way switch from the house or add more than one circuit. Use THWN-2 14-gauge stranded wire if you get power from a 15-amp circuit or THWN-2 12-gauge stranded wire for a 20-amp circuit. Leave enough extra wire on each end to reach the inside metal box plus 12 in.

The NEC requires a means, such as a single-pole switch, to disconnect the power where it enters the shed. Photo 9 shows how to connect the switch, ground wire and neutral wires. Run wires from the switch to a GFCI receptacle, and from there to the rest of the outlets or lights in your shed.

Apply heat-reducing window film

Heat control film is composed of treated micro-thin layers of film that block ultraviolet rays and reduce the summer heat that comes through the window.

Heat control window film will help keep a room cooler, and you can install it yourself. These films reflect the sun's heat and ultraviolet rays, and reduce glare without obscuring the view (see photo). The more direct sunlight coming through the window, the more the film will help (and it may lower your air-conditioning bills!).

Applying the film takes approximately 30 minutes per window (inset photo). The film should last about 10 years. Prices vary with film size and type of film. A 3-ft. x 15-ft. film (which can cover two to three windows) costs $30 to $50 and up, depending on type. The film is sold at home centers and hardware stores.

Different types of film are available, so get the one designed for heat control. The film can be applied to any window, including double-pane low-e windows, although they already reduce radiant heat loss and gain.

One drawback is that the film may void the manufacturer's warranty for the seal on double-pane windows, although the film shouldn't affect the seal. If the window warranty has already expired or reducing excessive heat is more important to you than possibly jeopardizing a warranty, then apply the film. Otherwise, consider other options, such as installing shades, awnings or shutters over the windows or even planting a tree on the west side to block the sun.

Window film can be installed in about 30 minutes. The hazy appearance will disappear after 10 days.

WHAT IT TAKES

Time: 30 minutes
Skill level: Beginner

Energy-saving weekend projects

Change your furnace filter

Keeping your furnace (gas or electric) tuned up has two big benefits: It makes the furnace run efficiently and it prolongs the furnace's life span. And you can perform the annual tune-up yourself in about three hours (search for "furnace" at familyhandyman.com).

Change the filter every month of the heating season (or year-round if the filter is also used for A/C). Be sure you insert the new one so it faces the right way. The filter protects the blower and its motor; a clogged filter makes the motor work harder and use more power.

Clean out the lint *for dryer efficiency*

A clogged lint screen or dryer duct drastically reduces the efficiency of your dryer, whether it's gas or electric. Clean the lint screen after each load and clean the exhaust duct once a year. The tool shown here has an auger brush that attaches to a drill to clean out the ducts. It's available at home centers.

Electric dryers use about $85 of electricity annually. A dirty lint screen can cause the dryer to use up to 30 percent more electricity, according to the Consumer Energy Center. Lint buildup is also a common cause of fires.

Dry loads of laundry back-to-back so the dryer doesn't cool down between loads (a warm dryer uses less energy). And only run the dryer until the clothes are dry. Overdrying damages your clothes and runs up your electric bill. If you're in the market for a new dryer and already have a gas line in the house, go with a gas dryer. A gas dryer is more efficient.

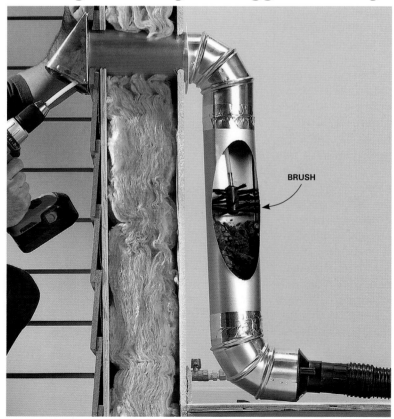

BRUSH

Keep your dryer safe and efficient by cleaning lint out of the ductwork once a year.

Service your air conditioner

Roughly half of an average home's annual energy bill (gas and electric), about $1,000, is spent on heating and cooling. Air conditioners placed in direct sunlight use up to 10 percent more electricity. If yours sits in the sun, plant tall shrubs or shade trees nearby—but don't enclose the unit or impede the airflow. Place window units on the north side of the house or install an awning over them.

Keep your window or central air conditioner tuned up so it runs at peak efficiency (search for "air conditioners" at familyhandyman.com to find out how to do it yourself). Every two or three years, call in a pro to check the electrical parts and the refrigerant (expect to pay $150 or more).

If your central air conditioner is more than 12 years old, replacing it with an Energy Star model can cut your cooling costs by 30 percent and save maintenance costs. The payback for replacing a 12-year-old system is typically about eight years. An air conditioner's efficiency level is measured by the seasonal energy efficiency ratio (SEER). The higher the number, the more efficient the unit. A 13 or 14 SEER rating is considered high efficiency.

The best way to keep your air conditioner running at peak efficiency is to spend a couple of hours each year on basic maintenance—cleaning and straightening the fins, changing the filter and lubricating the motor.

Run your refrigerator for less

Your refrigerator uses more electricity than all your other kitchen appliances combined. To keep its energy costs down, clean the coils twice a year, which improves efficiency by 30 to 50 percent.

Your fridge and freezer run more efficiently when they're full. Put water containers in the fridge and ice bags in your freezer to keep them filled. Keep the refrigerator setting between 35 and 38 degrees and the freezer between 0 and 5 degrees F.

Refrigerator door seals wear out over time. Test your seal by closing a dollar bill in the door. If it pulls out easily, replace the seal (search for "refrigerator seal" at familyhandyman.com).

Brush and vacuum the coils at the bottom or the back of the refrigerator. A coil cleaning brush (sold at home centers) is bendable to fit in tight areas.

If your fridge was made before 2001, it's using at least 40 percent more electricity than new Energy Star models. If you're replacing your fridge, buy an Energy Star model and recycle your old one (visit energystar.gov and search "refrigerator recycling" to find out how). Don't hook up the old one in the basement or garage—an inefficient refrigerator costs as much as $280 a year in electricity, according to the Consumer Energy Center. Any money you save buying food in bulk and storing it in an inefficient second fridge is lost in electric costs.

Fix your central A/C

You can't cool off in front of the open fridge forever. It's time to decide: You can either wait four days for the service guy to show up or try fixing your central air conditioner yourself. We'll show you which A/C failures can be handled by a DIYer and how to safely replace the three parts that cause the majority of all outdoor condenser unit failures. You'll need a standard multimeter, an insulated needle-nose pliers and ordinary hand tools.

We'll assume you've checked the A/C and furnace circuit breakers in the main electrical panel, as well as any cartridge fuses in the outside disconnect. Replace all three parts at once (about $150 total; see "Buy the Right Parts," p. 127). Of course, that might mean you'll replace some good parts. But if the fixes work, your A/C will be up and running much sooner and you'll save about $150. Or you can replace the parts one at a time and test the unit after each one.

If these fixes don't work, at least you've covered the most common failures, and your service guy can concentrate on finding the more elusive problem. Plus, with the new parts, you'll likely add years of breakdown-free air conditioning.

Make sure the problem isn't the furnace

Set your thermostat to A/C mode and lower the temperature setting. If the furnace fan kicks in, the problem isn't in the furnace. If the fan doesn't run, try resetting the furnace circuit breaker. If the fan still won't start, call a pro—the fixes shown here won't work.

Next, check the outside condensing unit. The compressor (which sounds like a refrigerator) and fan should be running. If not, follow the troubleshooting and repair procedures shown here.

Clean or replace the contactor relay

The contactor relay switches power to the condenser fan and the compressor. It rarely fails. But it often gets jammed with beetles, bugs and spiders that perished checking things out. Remove the condenser unit's access cover and locate the contactor relay—it'll have at least six wires attached to it. Try cleaning the critters out with compressed air (Photo 1). If that works, fine. But if you can't remove all the fried bug parts, replace the contactor

with a new unit (about $30). Don't think you can file the contacts to clean them. That fix won't last.

Replace the capacitor(s)

The "start" and "run" capacitors store electrical energy to jump-start the compressor and fan motor. You may have a combination start/run capacitor or two individual ones. Both styles have a very high failure rate, and when they go, the compressor or fan won't start. They're cheap (about $30), so replace them.

First discharge any remaining electrical charge from the capacitor(s) before you work on them. Fabricate a shorting resistor pack by twisting four 5.6k-ohm, 1/2-watt resistors in series. Then discharge the capacitor (Photo 2).

Next, move each wire lead from the old capacitor to the new capacitor (Photo 3).

> **CAUTION:** **Turn off the A/C and furnace breakers in the main electrical panel before pulling the outdoor disconnect or removing the condensing unit's access panel. Then use a voltage sniffer on the wires coming into the contactor to make sure the power is really off.**

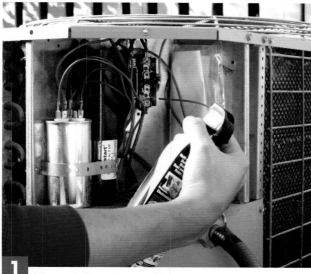

1 **Blow out the contactor.** Blow compressed air into all sides of the contactor relay to clean out dead insects. If you're not able to remove all the debris, you'll have to replace the contactor. Then try starting the unit.

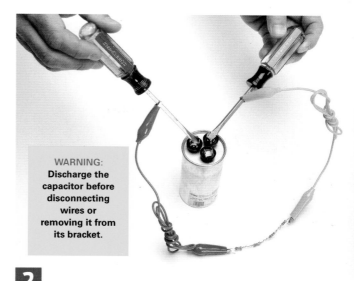

WARNING:
Discharge the capacitor before disconnecting wires or removing it from its bracket.

2 **Discharge the old capacitor.** Attach a jumper lead to each end of the resistor pack. Clip the other ends to insulated screwdrivers. Then touch the screwdrivers to the capacitor terminals.

3 **Swap capacitor wires to the new unit.** Wiggle each wire off the old capacitor, noting the terminal markings. Place the wire on the matching terminal on the new capacitor. Then secure the new capacitor in the mounting bracket.

4 **Install the new fan motor.** Align the fan motor studs with the holes in the fan guard or condenser cover. Then spin on the acorn nuts and tighten. Install the fan blade and the electrical connector. Tuck the new fan wires into the old conduit.

Replace the fan motor

Remove the fasteners that hold the fan guard in place or remove the entire cover assembly from the condenser unit. Lift out the fan assembly and mark the bottom of the blade so you replace it in the right direction. Then loosen the blade-retaining nut and pull it off the motor shaft. Disconnect the fan motor electrical connector. Then swap in the new fan motor (Photo 4). Reconnect the fan guard or condenser cover.

Check out the operation

Reinstall the access cover and the outside disconnect block. Raise the temperature on the thermostat. Then flip the A/C and furnace breakers to "On." Wait 15 minutes for the thermostat and furnace electronics to reset. Then lower the temperature setting. The condensing unit should start up. If it doesn't, your system may need more time to reset. Wait one hour and try it again. If it still doesn't work, schedule a service call. Be sure to specify exactly you did. That'll keep the repair person from replacing brand new parts, and you'll be able to have your work checked by an expert.

> ### Buy the right parts
> Buy replacement parts from your local appliance parts store or A/C dealer. You'll need the make, model and serial numbers from the nameplate on your outdoor condensing unit—not the furnace nameplate. Or, if you're willing to pay for overnight delivery, you can buy discount parts online.

Super-insulate your attic

Save $1,000 or more on labor and cut your heating bills

If you need to add insulation in your attic, save big by blowing in cellulose insulation yourself. Blowing attic insulation isn't hard, but it's dusty, sweaty work. To make it easier, enlist a helper and set aside two days: one for attic prep and the second to actually blow the insulation. By the end of the weekend you're going to be sore and tired. But saving $1,000 or more will make up for your aching back.

The long-term payoff is impressive too. You could see your energy bills go down by as much as 15 to 25 percent depending on your climate and existing levels of insulation.

1 Pull back the existing insulation and use expanding spray foam to seal any gaps around plumbing pipes, ceiling perforations and holes where electrical wires snake through. Make sure to seal all the way around the pipe. For gaps 1/4 in. or less, use caulk rather than expanding foam.

FOAM VENT CHUTES

2 Pull the existing insulation away from the roof. Position the new vent chute so the bottom extends 6 in. into the overhang and staple it into place. It's a good idea to use a squeeze stapler instead of a hammer stapler because it's more accurate and there's less chance you'll crumple the chute.

Day one

Seal attic bypasses

Leaks from cracks and gaps around lights, plumbing pipes, chimneys, walls and other ceiling penetrations are the equivalent of having a 2-ft.-wide hole in your ceiling. The worst offenders are open stud and joist cavities and dropped soffits and ceilings in kitchens and baths. You'll learn some basics here (Photo 1), but for complete step-by-step detailed information about how to seal attic bypasses, go to familyhandyman.com and type "seal attic air leaks" in the search box.

Install or repair vent chutes

In many homes, the vent chutes are missing or aren't properly installed. Without them, you're not getting the most out of your insulation's R-value because air needs to move properly at the eaves to remove moisture in the winter and heat in the summer.

To make sure existing chutes aren't blocked, stand in a dark attic to see whether light from the eaves is filtering through the vents. Replace any chutes that are blocked, damaged or missing. You'll find both plastic and foam vent chutes at home centers. Use foam chutes because they're more rigid and there's less chance of them getting crumpled or compressed when you're installing them. Pull back the existing insulation so you can see out to the edge of the eaves, and install a vent chute in every rafter space (Photo 2).

Dam and insulate the attic access

To keep the insulation from falling through the attic hatch opening, make a 2x12 dam around the hatch perimeter. Then, to really seal the attic access up tight, lay fiberglass batt insulation on the inside of the hatch or door and wrap it up tight like a Christmas present (Photo 3). You can insulate the hatch door while you're inside the attic or slide the door out and do it more comfortably on a tarp outside.

Mark your final insulation level

When you're blowing insulation, it can get dusty and hard to see whether you've got it deep enough around the entire attic. Mark the desired level on different roof trusses around the attic before you start (Photo 4).

Do you need to add insulation?

The answer depends on where you live, the heating and cooling costs in your area, your existing insulation levels, local codes and more. The first step is to make sure you've sealed your attic bypasses. Then do an Internet search for "Zip Code Insulation Tool." You'll find sites with calculators that use your zip code, and sometimes other data, to make recommendations.

The recommended insulation level for most attics is R-38 (or about 12 to 15 in. from the drywall, depending on the insulation type). In the coldest climates, insulating up to R-49 is recommended.

Day one

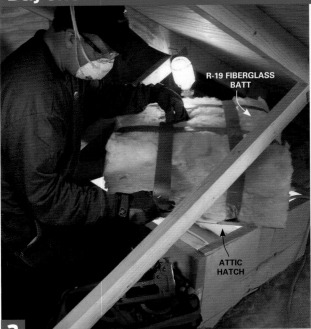

R-19 FIBERGLASS BATT

ATTIC HATCH

3 Cover the attic hatch with a pillow of fiberglass insulation. You want a nice, big puffy pillow of insulation to stop any air leaks. Cut two layers of R-19 fiberglass batt insulation slightly larger than the hatch and staple duct tape to the hatch edges to secure it in place.

DESIRED INSULATION LEVEL

4 Measure up from the ceiling to mark your desired insulation level. Use a permanent marker to mark the level every few trusses so you know you have even coverage around the entire space.

Day two

HOPPER DOOR

5 Have your helper crumble the compressed cellulose as he loads the hopper so it doesn't clog the hose. If the cellulose comes out too fast or too slow, adjust the hopper door. The blower machine is loud, and you and your assistant won't be in visual contact. Communicate with each other using a walkie-talkie or cell phone. You can also click the blower control switch on and off several times to get your helper's attention.

6 Start at the farthest point from the hatch and sit in the center of the attic. Don't move around a lot in the attic with the hose. Work from the middle and do three bays at a time. Push the hose out to the eaves and blow those areas first. Then pull the hose back and use a slow, steady sweeping motion until you reach the desired level. Then pivot in place and blow the opposite side of the attic the same way.

The 3 most common DIY insulation mistakes

Mistake #1: **Not sealing attic air leaks first**
No amount of insulation is going to help if you don't seal your attic properly. For detailed step-by-step information about sealing attic air leaks, go to familyhandyman.com and type "seal attic air leaks."

Mistake #2: **Not getting insulation out to the edges**
When you're prepping the attic, use a broom handle or stick to push the existing insulation out to the edges. Then when you blow in the cellulose, make sure you do a good job of getting it way over to the eaves with the hose.

Mistake #3: **Stepping through the ceiling**
It happens all the time. You've got to move around slowly and step from joist to joist. If there's no floor, bring up a 12-in.-wide piece of 3/4-in. plywood and lay it across the ceiling joists to use as a platform to work from. And wear rubber-soled shoes so you can feel the joists through the bottoms of your feet.

Day two

Pick up the blower and insulation

Cellulose insulation is a good choice for DIYers. It has a higher R-rating and is less expensive than either blown fiberglass or fiberglass batts. It's an environmentally friendly material made from recycled newspaper, so it's easier on your skin and lungs. And you can blow it easily and quickly into odd-shaped spaces in an attic, where access is limited and dragging up batts is tough.

Most home centers sell bagged cellulose insulation, and many provide the blower for a minimal fee or free when you buy a certain number of bags (usually 10 or more). You can also rent the blowers from a rental center. Although rental machines aren't as powerful as the truck-mounted units the pros use, they work fine for a DIYer.

To determine how many bags you'll need, measure your existing insulation so you know your current R-value and subtract that from the recommended levels (see "Do You Need to Add Insulation?" on p. 129 for how to find recommended levels for your zip code). Check the chart on the insulation bag to determine the number of bags necessary to reach your desired R-value based on the square footage of your attic. Buy more bags than you think you'll need. You can always return them, and you don't want to stop in the middle of the job because you've run out.

Set up the blower

The blower machine is heavy, so have your helper along to help you load and unload it. Set the blower on a tarp on flat ground near the window or vent opening closest to the attic access. Your helper will feed the insulation into the hopper while you work the hose up in the attic (Photo 5).

The blower should include two 50-ft. hoses that you can connect and snake into the attic. If your hoses have to wind their way through the house to reach a scuttle (the attic access) in a hallway or closet, lay down tarps along the way. It keeps things neater during the process and makes cleanup a lot easier.

Connect the hoses with the coupler and then use duct tape over the coupler to secure the connection. The metal clamps can vibrate themselves loose. You don't want them to get disconnected and have cellulose sprayed all around your house.

Blow the insulation

Wear eye protection, a long-sleeve shirt and gloves, and a double-strap mask or particulate respirator. Start as far away from the access panel as possible and blow the eaves and other tight spots first. For hard-to-reach areas, duct tape a length of PVC pipe to the end of the blower hose. As you work back into corners and around eave vents, don't cover any ventilating areas.

You can blow three rafter bays on each side of the attic from one position. Let the hose sit on the drywall to fill the eave areas, giving it a shake to move it from bay to bay. For the center areas, hold the hose level and blow the insulation evenly until you've reached your level lines (Photo 6). Then pivot in place and do the same thing to the other side. Move across the attic until you've hit your desired height at every point. Blow the rest of the insulation until the hopper is empty. You'll end up with a clean blower, and the extra inch or two of insulation will settle over the next few months.

Cut down a tree

Learn how to make it fall where you want it

It would be hard to name a more dangerous DIY project than felling a big tree.

There's the obvious risk of getting crushed by a falling tree, but you could also have your melon crushed if a big limb shook loose from above. Trees can twist as they fall and make all kinds of other unexpected moves. Add a chain saw to the mix, and—well, you get the idea. It's not a job for the careless, the reckless or the faint-of-heart.

There are some commonsense precautions you should take and techniques you should employ to make tree felling as safe as possible. We'll share those with you. We'll also tell you how to analyze the situation so you'll know when it's best to call in a pro.

Aside from a chain saw, a stiff dose of common sense and a bit of courage, you'll need a few things to properly fell a tree. They include safety gear (see "The Right Stuff," at right) and two plastic felling wedges to keep your saw from getting pinched in cuts on larger trees. You can find everything you'll need at any outdoor power equipment store that carries chain saws. Don't bother looking for these items at home centers.

Felling wedges ($10 to $15): These wedges will prevent your saw from getting pinched during a cut.

The right stuff

Safety isn't a throwaway word when it comes to felling trees and running chain saws. You must take it seriously. There are a few absolutely essential safety gear items you need to wear for any chain saw work.

Loggers helmet ($30 to $80): The helmet protects you from falling branches, a major cause of logging injuries. Earmuffs and a face screen protect your ears and eyes. Safety glasses keep the dust out—you don't want something in your eye in the middle of dropping a 4-ft.-diameter cottonwood.

Kevlar chaps ($50 to $80): Kevlar fibers will stop a chain instantly should you happen to drop the bar against your leg. It's the best logging safety device developed in the past 30 years, and it's a rare (and foolish) pro who doesn't wear them.

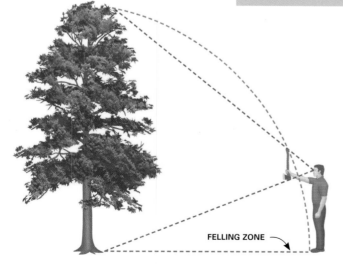

FELLING ZONE

Estimate the felling zone

Trees are taller than you think and reach farther on the ground than you'd expect (maybe all the way to your shed). You can estimate where a tree will fall by using the "ax handle trick." Hold an ax handle at arm's length, close one eye, and back away from or move toward the tree until the top of the ax is even with the treetop and the bottom even with the base. Your feet should be about where the treetop will rest after falling. It's just an estimate, though, so allow extra room if there's something it might fall on!

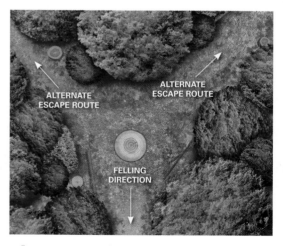

ALTERNATE ESCAPE ROUTE

ALTERNATE ESCAPE ROUTE

FELLING DIRECTION

Clear a cutting zone

Even when you're sure which way the tree is going to fall, you're still not ready to fell it. Cut away any brush around the trunk and clear two escape routes on the "non-falling" side of the tree. They should be about 45 degrees away from each other in opposite directions. The last thing you want is to trip while walking away from a falling tree.

Anatomy of a proper notch

The rule of thumb is to make the depth of the notch one-fifth of the tree trunk's diameter. The goal is to make the angles as shown in the diagram (or as close as you can). The felling cut should meet the point of the notch. When the tree starts to fall, the hinge will help guide the tree to fall in the desired direction.

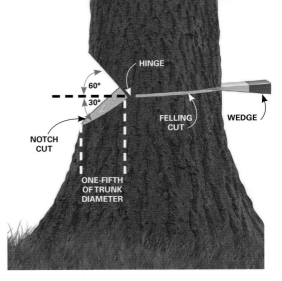

HINGE

60°
30°

NOTCH CUT

FELLING CUT

WEDGE

ONE-FIFTH OF TRUNK DIAMETER

Size up the tree

Start by studying the crown of the tree. Look for dead branches that are broken but attached, or actually broken off and supported by other branches. Don't even think about cutting down the tree yourself if you see any danger upstairs. You're bound to knock a branch loose and have it fall on you.

Next look at the lean and the branch loading. If it's obviously leaning in one direction or heavily loaded with branches on one side, that's the way it's going to fall. Forget the myth that a pro can drop a tree on top of an empty beer can. If it's perfectly straight and evenly loaded—maybe he'll get close. But if it's loaded or leaning, he won't have a chance.

Are there any buildings, fences, power lines or other things you care about in the felling zone? If so, skip the felling and call a pro.

NOTCH LOCATION

Plan the notch

You're going to be cutting a notch on the "fall" side of the trunk. Sight along the handle and adjust the saw until it's pointing toward your fall direction. The spot where the bar touches the bark will be the center of the notch. Before cutting, lay out the notch by marking with chalk or by scoring the bark with the chain saw. Make the notch at a comfortable working height. (You can always shorten the stump later.)

NOTCH

Cut the notch

Make the top cut first and then the bottom. When you're making the bottom cut, adjust your hand to control the throttle with your thumb. If you meet the top notch perfectly, the wedge will drop out of the notch. But most likely you'll have to extend the cuts from either the top or the bottom so the wedge can drop free.

FELLING CUT

Use wedges on big trees

If you have a tree that's more than 18 in. in diameter, go ahead and make your notch cut and begin the felling cut. Stop cutting as soon as you've penetrated far enough to pound wedges behind the bar. Leave the bar in the cut with the saw running, but lock the chain brake and tap in the wedges. Then finish the cut. Wedges will keep the saw from getting pinched in the cut if the tree leans back.

Tree-dropping wisdom

- Never cut on a breezy day.
- You'll have an easier time cutting up a fallen tree if you do it when the leaves are missing.
- Grab the chain saw handle with an encircling thumb on your right hand and never release it during a cut.
- Stay away from hollowed-out trees, especially if they're big. They are extremely unpredictable and dangerous to fell.
- Gas up the saw before beginning a cut. Never run out of gas halfway through a cut.
- Once you start working, don't stop until the tree is down. You don't want the tree to fall while you're taking a break.

FELLING CUT

Make the felling cut

Score a line connecting the apex of the notch on both sides for a cutting guide. The back cut should be parallel and even with the apex of the notch. Then make the felling cut. The instant the tree begins leaning, pull the saw free, set the chain brake and walk away along one of your escape routes, keeping an eye on the tree so you can react if it doesn't fall the way you planned. Never take your eye off a falling tree.

A lookout might save your life

You'll be a lot safer if you have a trusted assistant standing a few feet behind you watching the top of the tree for falling branches and letting you know when the tree starts to fall. Have your assistant tap you on the shoulder with a stick to alert you when it's time to vacate the area. If it's early in the cut and you get the tap, leave the saw and walk away immediately. That means a branch is falling. Near the end of the cut, a tap means the tree is beginning its descent.

Ultimate wall system *in a (long) weekend*

Flexible garage storage that you can build with just a circular saw and a drill

The problem with organizing garages is that there are so many different kinds of things to store that it's overwhelming trying to decide how to do it. But with this system, you don't have to worry about the ultimate positioning of all your hooks and shelves because you can rearrange them at will. And you don't have to plan ahead for future storage needs either. You can easily add on to the system just by assembling more hangers and rearranging the existing ones. Once the beveled strips are attached, you never have to locate a stud or use drywall anchors to hang hooks or other hardware. Just screw them to an appropriate-size wood-cleat hanger and put them up wherever you want.

The system consists of beveled strips that are screwed to the wall studs, and custom-made wooden hangers that lock onto the strips. We built everything with utility plywood, which costs about $45 a sheet. You can cut enough strips from a 4 x 8-ft. sheet to cover a 12-ft.-long

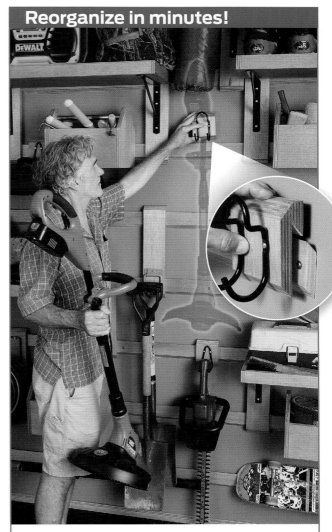

Reorganize in minutes!

Rearrange, reorganize, add on, make room for new stuff. It's as easy as lifting off the hangers and putting them somewhere else. There's nothing complicated about this storage system. The matching bevels and gravity hold the hangers securely until you want to move them. And you can build the whole system with just two power tools—a circular saw and a drill. What could be simpler!

WHAT IT TAKES Time: 2–3 days Skill level: Beginner

wall. And you can assemble enough hangers, tool totes and other miscellaneous holders from another 4 x 8 sheet to get a good start on organizing your garage. See the Materials List on p. 139 for other items you may need. We used four sheets of plywood to build everything you see in the photo.

It would be a little quicker to cut the parts using a table saw and a miter saw, but you don't need these tools; we'll show you how to safely and accurately cut all the parts using just a circular saw. You'll be surprised at how quickly and easily you can cut the parts with the help

Build a saw guide for perfect cuts

To make the saw guide, start by marking a line and cutting a 5-in.-wide strip from the edge of an uncut sheet of plywood (photo below left). You could simply clamp this straightedge to the plywood as a saw guide, but then you would have to compensate for the distance from the guide to the saw blade every time. The photo below right shows how to build a guide that you can line up with the cutting mark, a technique that is quicker and more accurate.

Make another guide just like this one, except set the saw to cut 90 degrees when you cut off the excess 1/4-in. plywood. You can use the opposite edge of the same sheet of plywood for the straight edge. Use this guide for non-beveled cuts.

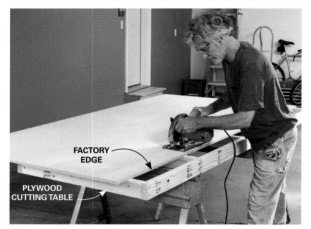

Make a straightedge. Saw off the factory edge of a sheet of plywood to use as a straightedge. It doesn't matter if you don't saw perfectly straight because you'll only use the factory edge. Draw arrows toward the factory edge to identify it.

Build the guide. Attach a 12-in.-wide strip of 1/4-in. plywood to the straightedge with short screws. Make sure to face the factory edge of the straightedge toward the excess base material. Then, with the saw set to a 45-degree bevel, run the saw's bed along the straightedge to cut off the excess base. Make a second guide using the opposite edge of the 4 x 8 sheet of plywood, only set the saw to cut 90 degrees.

Build these simple guides for cutting the small parts

Both of these crosscut guides are simple: All you need to do is glue a 1-3/8-in.-wide strip of plywood or MDF to a wider strip. Set the workpiece on the guide, clamp on a rafter square and run your saw along the square to get straight, precise cuts. This works for plain cuts or 45-degree bevels. It's best to have two widths and two sizes of rafter squares for different size parts.

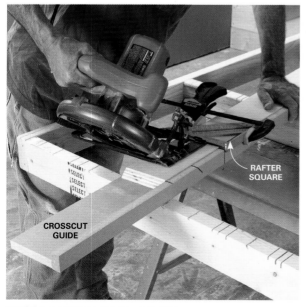

Build a narrow crosscut guide

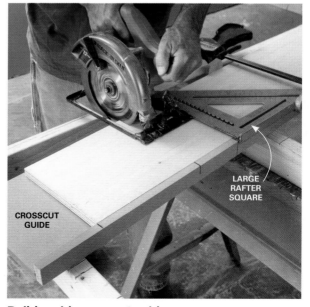

Build a wide crosscut guide

of a few simple saw guides. But before you start, make sure you have a sharp blade for your circular saw. To make clean, splinter-free cuts in plywood, buy a 40-tooth carbide blade. In addition to a circular saw and drill, you'll need a hammer, level, tape measure, pair of clamps, chalk line with dust-off chalk, and small and large rafter squares.

Screw the strips to the wall

Cut the strips from a sheet of plywood. Photo 1 shows how. You won't be able to cut the narrow beveled strips from the last 10 or 12 in. of the plywood sheet with this guide. Instead, use the remaining wide strip for the totes or other wider parts.

Next, to ensure that the strips are straight and level and that all the screws hit the center of the studs, make a grid of chalk lines. Start by drawing a level line to mark the bottom of the lowest strip (Photo 2). Then make marks every 12 in. above the line and connect the marks with chalk lines (Photo 3). Use special dust-off chalk—it's easily erasable.

Next, locate the center of a stud. Use a stud finder or knock on the wall until you feel and hear a solid spot. Then zero in on the center by probing with a nail (Photo 4). Do this above the lines, where the nail holes will be covered by the strips. Find both edges of the stud with the nail. Then mark the center. In most cases, studs are 16 in. apart, and you can measure from this first center mark to find the remaining studs. Whatever method you use, probe with a nail at each stud to make sure you hit solid wood. Make marks for the center of the studs at the top and bottom and connect the marks with chalk lines. With the grid done, it's easy to align and attach the strips (Photo 5).

Cut out the parts for the hangers

With the saw guides, it's fast and easy to make long, table saw–quality cuts in plywood. But what about all those small parts? One problem with cutting small parts freehand is that it's hard to keep the cuts square. Another is that the cutoff pieces tend to fall away just before the cut is finished, creating a little torn-off section. You can solve both these problems,

1 Cut beveled strips. Start by positioning the beveled guide 1 in. from the edge and cutting a strip with a bevel on one edge. You can use this to make hangers. Then make a series of marks 2-1/2 in. apart on each end of the sheet. Line up the saw guide with the marks to cut the beveled strips.

2 Mark a level line. Measure up from the floor 9 in. and make a mark. Use a straight board and a level to draw a level line.

Materials list

Here's what we used. Adjust the quantities for your project.

ITEM	QTY.	ITEM	QTY.
2' x 4' x 3/4" MDF (crosscut guides)	1	1-1/4" construction screws (to attach cleats to hangers)	100
2' x 8' x 1/4" plywood or hardboard (saw guide base)	1	1-3/4" construction screws (optional—for cabinets)*	100
4' x 8' x 3/4" plywood	4	2-3/4" construction screws* (to attach cleats to wall)	175
No. 4 x 3/4" wood screws (to attach 1/4" plywood to straightedge for guide)	20	8-oz. bottle of wood glue	1
7/8" pan-head screws (to attach hardware to cleats)	100	3/4" copper tubing (optional)	
		Hooks and other hardware**	

*We used premium, self-tapping No. 8 cabinet screws. Find them at home centers or online.

**We used the a hook assortment pack, flip-up tool holder and flip-up bike holder, available at home centers.

and make marks for repeatable cuts, by building two crosscut guides (p. 138). We bought a 2 x 4-ft. piece of MDF at the home center, but you can use any flat scraps of plywood.

Start by cutting two fence strips 1-3/8 in. wide by 3 or 4 ft. long. Then cut a 4-1/2-in.-wide strip and a 9-1/2-in.-wide strip for the base pieces. Use your straightedge saw guide to make these cuts. Glue and clamp the fence parts to the base pieces. Or you can glue and screw them. If you use screws, remove them after the glue sets.

The sidebar on p. 138 shows how to use the crosscut guides. When you make the first cut, mark the location of the square on the crosscut guide. To make several parts that are the same length, measure from the saw kerf in the work support and make a mark. Line up the end of the material with this mark and align the clamp with the clamp mark.

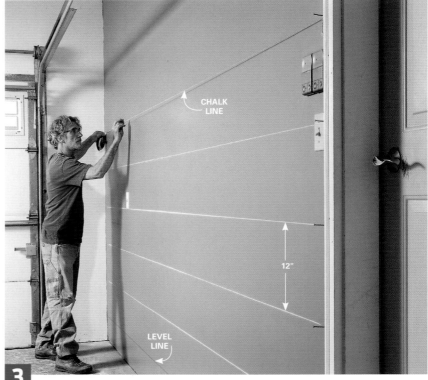

3 **Mark the cleat locations with chalk lines.** Measure up from the level line and make marks every 12 in. Do this on both ends. Then snap chalk lines between the marks. Use dust-off chalk, which won't leave permanent stains on the wall.

4 **Mark the center of the studs.** Locate a stud with a finder or the knuckle-knocking method. Then probe with a nail until you find both edges of the stud. Mark the center of the stud. Measure from this mark—most studs are 16 in. center-to-center—to find the remaining stud centers. Double-check by probing with a nail at each mark. Repeat this process at the uppermost chalk line and connect the marks with chalk lines.

5 **Screw the strips to the studs.** Line up the bottom of the strips with the lines and drive a screw into each stud. We used washer-head cabinet screws, but any type of screw will work.

Go crazy!

We've shown you how to mount the strips and cut out parts for the simple hangers. But with a little ingenuity, you can hang just about anything from these beveled strips. The golf bag holder and tote boxes are just a few ideas. We haven't included detailed plans because frankly, it doesn't really matter. Anything you can attach to a beveled cleat is fair game. Home centers, hardware stores and sporting goods stores all have hooks and brackets for hanging stuff. You just have to build a wooden cleat to screw them to. Have something to hang? Have fun inventing a new hanging bracket. When you're finished, your garage will be the envy of the neighborhood.

CLEAT | **45° BEVEL**

1-3/4"

Long hangers
These are like the small ones, only long enough to rest on the horizontal cleat below. Use these for shelf brackets and other longer hardware.

16-1/2"

4"

Small hangers
Glue and screw the small cleat to the back of the face. Drill pilot holes for the screws.

4"

4-1/2"

Golf bag holder
This is just one example of a custom holder you can build. You could even build cabinets hung by cleats. They're easier to hang and you can move them around if you want to change the design.

2"

36"

7"

11-1/2"

17-1/2"

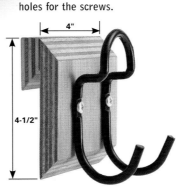

2"

10"

6-1/2"

9"

13-1/2"

Wooden totes
Build plywood boxes and attach cleats to the back. We drilled 7/8-in. holes, 1/2 in. deep in the ends with a Forstner bit to hold the 3/4-in. copper tubing handles.

Garden storage closet

If you don't have room in your yard for a large, freestanding shed, you can still create plenty of space for garden tools with a shed attached to the back or side of the house. If you're an experienced builder, you can build this shed in a couple of weekends. The one shown cost about $400, but you could save about $75 by using treated lumber, pine, and asphalt shingles instead of cedar.

Frame the walls and roof

Nail together the side walls, then square them with the plywood side panels. Overhang the panels 3/8 in. at the front—this will hide the gap at the corner when you hang the doors.

Join the two sides with the top and bottom plates and rim joists. The sides, top and bottom are all mirror images of each other except for the top front rim joist, which is set down 1/2 in. from the top so it stops the doors (Photo 1). Use screws to fasten the framework together except in the front where fasteners will be visible—use 2-1/2-in. casing nails there.

WHAT IT TAKES

Time: 2 weekends
Skill level: Intermediate

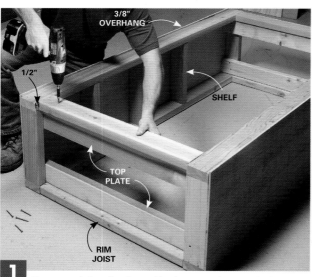

1 Frame and sheathe the walls, then join them with plates and joists. Use the best pieces of lumber in the front where they'll show.

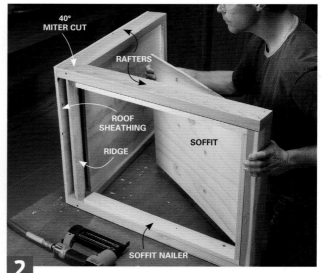

2 Build the roof on your workbench. Start with an L-shaped 2x4 frame, then add the nailers, soffit, sheathing and trim. Shingle with cedar or asphalt shingles.

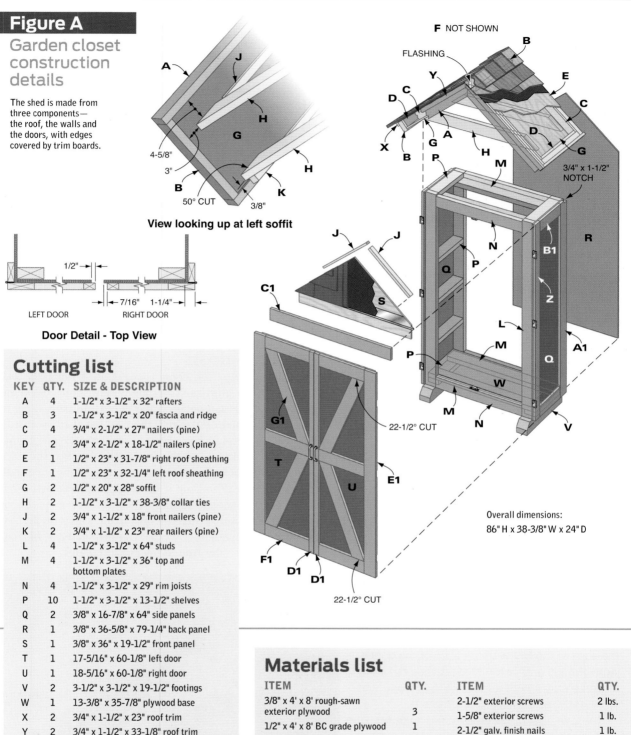

Figure A

Garden closet construction details

The shed is made from three components— the roof, the walls and the doors, with edges covered by trim boards.

View looking up at left soffit

4-5/8"
3"
50° CUT
3/8"

F NOT SHOWN
FLASHING

3/4" x 1-1/2" NOTCH

1/2"
7/16" 1-1/4"
LEFT DOOR   RIGHT DOOR

Door Detail - Top View

22-1/2° CUT

22-1/2° CUT

Overall dimensions:
86" H x 38-3/8" W x 24" D

Cutting list

KEY	QTY.	SIZE & DESCRIPTION
A	4	1-1/2" x 3-1/2" x 32" rafters
B	3	1-1/2" x 3-1/2" x 20" fascia and ridge
C	4	3/4" x 2-1/2" x 27" nailers (pine)
D	2	3/4" x 2-1/2" x 18-1/2" nailers (pine)
E	1	1/2" x 23" x 31-7/8" right roof sheathing
F	1	1/2" x 23" x 32-1/4" left roof sheathing
G	2	1/2" x 20" x 28" soffit
H	2	1-1/2" x 3-1/2" x 38-3/8" collar ties
J	2	3/4" x 1-1/2" x 18" front nailers (pine)
K	2	3/4" x 1-1/2" x 23" rear nailers (pine)
L	4	1-1/2" x 3-1/2" x 64" studs
M	4	1-1/2" x 3-1/2" x 36" top and bottom plates
N	4	1-1/2" x 3-1/2" x 29" rim joists
P	10	1-1/2" x 3-1/2" x 13-1/2" shelves
Q	2	3/8" x 16-7/8" x 64" side panels
R	1	3/8" x 36-5/8" x 79-1/4" back panel
S	1	3/8" x 36" x 19-1/2" front panel
T	1	17-5/16" x 60-1/8" left door
U	1	18-5/16" x 60-1/8" right door
V	2	3-1/2" x 3-1/2" x 19-1/2" footings
W	1	13-3/8" x 35-7/8" plywood base
X	2	3/4" x 1-1/2" x 23" roof trim
Y	2	3/4" x 1-1/2" x 33-1/8" roof trim
Z	2	3/4" x 2-1/2" x 64" side battens
A1	2	3/4" x 3-1/2" x 64" rear side battens
B1	4	3/4" x 3-1/2" x 11-1/8" horizontal side battens
C1	1	3/4" x 3-1/2" x 38-3/8" front trim
D1	2	3/4" x 1-1/2" x 60-1/8" door edge
E1	2	3/4" x 3-1/2" x 60-1/8" door edge
F1	6	3/4" x 3-1/2" x 14-1/8" horizontal door trim
G1	4	3/4" x 3-1/2" x 28-3/8" (long edge to long edge) diagonal door trim

Materials list

ITEM	QTY.	ITEM	QTY.
3/8" x 4' x 8' rough-sawn exterior plywood	3	2-1/2" exterior screws	2 lbs.
1/2" x 4' x 8' BC grade plywood	1	1-5/8" exterior screws	1 lb.
1x2 x 8' pine	1	2-1/2" galv. finish nails	1 lb.
1x2 x 8' cedar	3	1-1/2" galv. finish nails	1 lb.
1x3 x 8' pine	2	1" narrow crown staples (for cedar shingles)	1 lb.
1x3 x 8' cedar	2	30-lb. felt	1 roll
1x4 x 8' cedar	7	10" x 10' roll aluminum flashing	1 roll
Cedar shakes	1 bundle	2-1/2" x 2-1/2" rust-resistant hinges	3 prs.
2x4 x 8' cedar	11	Magnetic catches	1 pr.
4x4 x 4' pressure treated	1	Handles	1 pr.

Note: Shown are rough-sawn cedar boards—which usually (but not always!) measure 7/8 in. thick—for the trim. If you substitute pine, which measures 3/4 in., subtract 1/8 in. from each door width.

3 Set the completed roof on the shed base. Screw on the front and back panels to join the roof and the base.

ROOFING FELT

1" MINIMUM OVERLAP

FLASHING

4 Cover the front panel with roofing felt and shingles. Place metal flashing over the trim so water won't seep behind it.

Screw the 4x4 footings to the bottom plates, then nail on the plywood base. Cut and screw together the two pairs of rafters, then nail on the fascia and ridge boards. Nail on the roof sheathing and the soffit, butting the corners together (Photo 2). Screw on the collar ties at the points shown in Figure A, then screw on the front and rear nailers. Nail on the roof trim, staple on a layer of roofing felt, then shingle the roof. If you use cedar shingles, fasten them with narrow crown staples or siding nails. Leave 1/8-in. to 1/4-in. gaps between cedar shingles for expansion, and nail a strip of aluminum flashing across the ridge under the cap shingles.

Tip the shed upright, then set the roof on, aligning the front collar tie with the front rim joist and centering it side to side (Photo 3). Nail the cedar trim to the sides, aligning the 1x3s on the sides with the overhanging edge of plywood along the front edge. Glue and screw on the back and front siding panels to join the roof and base together. Use the back panel to square the structure and make it rigid.

Nail on the front trim piece, aligning it with the horizontal side battens (Z). Attach flashing and felt to the front panel, then cover it with cedar shakes (Photo 4).

Hang the doors

Finally, construct the doors (see Figure A detail, p. 143), cut the hinge mortises (see below) and hang the doors. Leave a 1/8-in. gap between the doors and trim along the top. Paint or stain if desired, then set the shed against the house on several inches of gravel. Add or take away gravel under the footings until the shed is tight against the siding and the gap above the doors is even. Screw the shed to the studs in the wall to keep it from tipping. Drill two 1/2-in. holes for the screws through the plywood near the rim joists, then loosely fasten the shed to the wall with 2-1/2-in. screws and large fender washers so the shed can move up and down when the ground freezes and thaws.

How to mortise a hinge

Mark the hinge locations on the door jamb, then on the door, less 1/8 in. for clearance at the top of the door. Separate the hinge leaves, then align the edge of the leaf with the edge of the door or jamb. Predrill and fasten the leaf, then cut along all three edges with a razor knife to about the same depth as the hinge leaf (Photo 1).

Remove the hinge and make a series of angled cuts to establish the depth of the mortise (Photo 2). Turn the chisel over and clean out the chips using light hammer taps.

Holding the chisel with the beveled front edge against the wood, chip out the 1/4-in. sections. Check the fit of the hinge leaf and chisel out additional wood until the leaf sits flush.

If the hinges don't fit back together perfectly when you hang the door, tap the leaves up or down (gently) with a hammer.

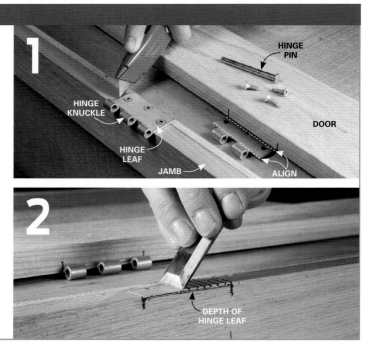

1

HINGE PIN

HINGE KNUCKLE

HINGE LEAF

JAMB

DOOR

ALIGN

2

DEPTH OF HINGE LEAF